THE ONE BIG BOOK

GRADE 2

For English, Math, and Science

★ Includes Math, English, Science - all in one colorful book

★ Detailed instructions to teach and learn with pictures and examples

★ Best book for home schooling, practicing, and teaching

★ Includes answers with detailed explanations

www.aceacademicpublishing.com

Author: Ace Academic Publishing

Prepaze is a sister company of Ace Academic Publishing. Intrigued by the unending possibilities of the internet and its role in education, Prepaze was created to spread the knowledge and learning across all corners of the world through an online platform. We equip ourselves with state-of-the-art technologies so that knowledge reaches the students through the quickest and the most effective channels.

The materials for our books are written by award winning teachers with several years of teaching experience. All our books are aligned with the state standards and are widely used by many schools throughout the country.

For enquiries and bulk order, contact us at the following address:

3736, Fallon Road, #403
Dublin, CA 94568
www.aceacademicpublishing.com

Ace Academic Publishing
ACHIEVING EXCELLENCE TOGETHER

This book contains copyright material. The purchase of this material entitles the buyer to use this material for personal and classroom use only. Reproducing the content for commercial use is strictly prohibited. Contact us to learn about options to use it for an entire school district or other commercial use.

ISBN: 978-1-949383-36-2
© Ace Academic Publishing, 2019

Other books from Ace Academic Publishing

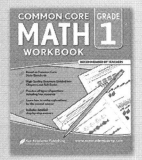 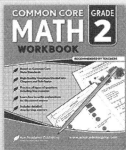 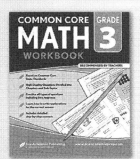 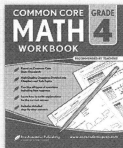 

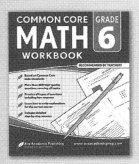 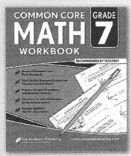 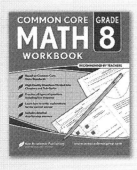  

  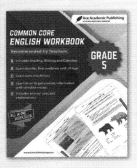  

Ace Academic Publishing
ACHIEVING EXCELLENCE TOGETHER

Other books from Ace Academic Publishing

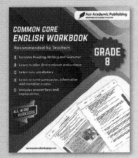    

Ace Academic Publishing
ACHIEVING EXCELLENCE TOGETHER

CONTENTS

ENGLISH

Language	2
Collective Nouns	2
Irregular Plural Nouns	6
Irregular Verbs	9
Adjectives	11
Adverbs	18
Capitalization	21
Commas	24
Apostrophes	26
Spelling Patterns	29
Context Clues	33
Root Words	38
Compound Words	40
Shades of Meanings	43

Reading: Informational Text	56
Trees	56
Cats or Dogs	58
Pizza	62
Life Cycle of a Hen	66

Reading: Foundational Skills	69
Long and Short Vowels	69
Two-Syllable Words	78
Prefixes and Suffixes	80

Reading: Literature	45
Unity Is Strength	45
A Visit to the Farmhouse	48
Mother Earth	51
The Rainbow	53

Writing	84
Opinion Writing	84
Explanatory Writing	86
Narrative Writing	87

www.prepaze.com

prepaze

MATH

Operations and Algebraic Thinking — 92

Odd and Even Numbers	93
Odd or even	93
Dot patterns	95
Smiley math	95
Arrays	96
Decorate with balloons	96
Skip count	96
Cupcakes and lego blocks	99
The flower pot problem	104
Who won the game?	105
Spot the odd one	106
Let's play a math game	108

Numbers and Operations in base 10 — 109

Representation of Numbers	109
Hundreds, tens, and ones	110
Who is missing?	113
Regroup	114
Skip count	114
Number bonds fun	117
Comparison of Numbers	119
Who is the greatest?	120
Pens and ice creams	121
Addition and Subtraction	124
Break apart	124
Solve using blocks	129
Is William correct?	133
True or false	133
Number colouring	136
Who am I?	137

www.prepaze.com

Measurement and Data	**143**
Measuring and Estimating Length	145
How long am I?	145
Ruler or yardstick	146
Riddle time	148
Home fun	152
Math fact	153
Inches, feet, meters, or centimeters?	153
Order me	154
Math with paper planes	157
Monday or Tuesday?	158
Time	166
Analogue and digital clocks	167
AM or PM	169
Money	169
Penny, quarter, nickel, or dime	169
Data	173
Oranges, apples, and pomegranate	173
Favorite pet	175
Sam's snack corner	176
What's your favourite musical instrument?	180

Geometry	**182**
Shapes	183
Square corners	184
Corners and sides	185
Complete me!	186
Am I congruent?	187
Equal Shares	187
Coloring fun	188
This or that?	189
Equal shares	191
Pizza math	192

SCIENCE

Physical Sciences	196
Movement of objects	196
Position of objects	196
Types of Force	197
Force	198
Effects of Force	198
Magnets	199
Magnetic Force	199
Scavenger Hunt for Magnets	200
Attraction or Repulsion?	201
Simple Machines	202
Types of Simple Machines	202
Simple Machines Around Us	203
Gravity	203
True or False?	204
Did you know?	205
Sound Energy	205
Types of Sounds	205
Sounds Around Us	206
Friction	207
Gravity Vs Friction	207
Uses of Friction	208
Energy Word Grid	209

Life Sciences	210
Name the Young ones	210
Animals and their Young ones	211
Reproduction in Animals	212
Did you know?	213
Reproduction in Plants	213
Lifecycle of a Butterfly	214
Lifecycle of a Frog	215
Did you know?	215
Rainforest Vs Desert	216
Structure of Plants	217
Taking After Parents	218
Germination	219
Lifecycle of a Plant	220
Seed Dispersal	220
Modes of Seed Dispersal	221

Earth Sciences	222
What are rocks made of?	222
Minerals	222
Identify the Minerals	223
Properties of Minerals	224
Agents of Weathering	225
Composition of Soil	226
Kinds of Soil	228
Fossils	229
Fossil Questionnaire	229
DIY Fossil	230
Did you know?	231
Natural Resources	231
Sources of Food	232
Uses of Natural Resources	233

Investigation and Experimentation	234
Make a Recipe card	234
Routine Journal	235
Bar Graph	236
Make Predictions	237

Answer Keys 239

www.prepaze.com

prepaze

English

This book enables your children to explore the English language and develop the necessary expertise. A series of thought-provoking exercises, engaging activities, and engrossing puzzles facilitate your children with understanding the intricacies of the English language.

Collective Nouns

Nouns are naming words for people, places, animals or things. A collective noun refers to a group or collection of people or things.

Examples

a bunch of keys

a hive of bees

a flock of birds

Unscramble the Words

Rearrange the scrambled letters to make collective nouns.

1. PDO _____
2. WRAMS _____
3. ACPK _____
4. RHED _____
5. HIGLTF _____
6. SHOLOC _____
7. BOROD _____
8. EAGLGG _____
9. LITERT _____
10. BOCKL _____

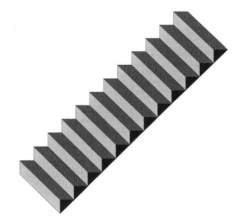

Pair It Up

Match the collective nouns to the respective nouns.

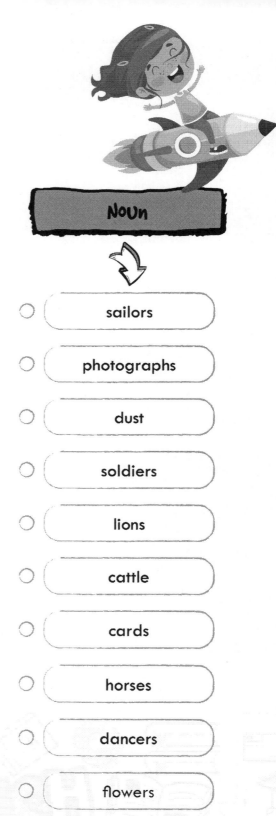

Collective Noun	Noun
army	sailors
pride	photographs
stud	dust
album	soldiers
cloud	lions
crew	cattle
group	cards
bouquet	horses
pack	dancers
herd	flowers

Choose the Best Answer

1. The school hired a _____ (crew/band) of musicians for the party.

2. We saw a _____ (flock/group) of sheep in the fields.

3. She climbed a long _____ (troop/flight) of stairs.

4. A _____ (pack/pod) of dolphins swam past the ship.

5. The players of our _____ (team/bunch) played well.

Irregular Plural Nouns

Most plurals are formed by adding s or es to the end of the word, but there are a few words whose plurals are irregular. That is, the spelling of a word or sometimes the word itself changes in plural form.

Another set of irregular plurals comprises words that have absolutely no change in spelling when used in the plural form.

Examples

Regular Plural Nouns

Singular	Plural
book	books
brush	brushes
dress	dresses
fox	foxes
orange	oranges

Examples

Irregular Plural Nouns

Singular	Plural
child	children
mouse	mice
deer	deer
sheep	sheep

Underline the Plural Nouns

1. Pete cleaned his desk and put the books on the shelves.

2. The trees shed leaves during fall.

3. Ron has lost four pens so far.

4. I always brush my teeth before going to bed.

5. The monkeys were swinging on the branch.

Make Plural Nouns

Use the plural form of the words in the parentheses.

1. He was lucky to get another chance to roll the _____ (die).

2. These _____ (woman) participated in the beauty pageant.

3. In some parts of the world, carts are pulled by _____ (ox).

4. She brought mashed _____ (potato) for the potluck.

5. The _____ (puppy) were happy to see their mother.

6. The _____ (glass) at the restaurant were unclean.

7. Mira is making _____ (pouch) for mobile phones.

8. I spotted colorful _____ (fish) in the tank.

9. The _____ (toy) were scattered on the floor.

10. Some _____ (goose) fly to warmer places during winter.

www.prepaze.com

Draw 4 nouns and color them. Label each drawing.

Irregular Verbs

Verbs or action words make up an important part of a sentence. Any verb formed by adding –d or –ed to the word while changing tense is said to be a regular verb.

Example: share, shared; walk, walked

The verbs that change forms when used in singular to plural or present to past or vice versa, are called irregular verbs.

Example: go, went; say, said;

There are also irregular verbs that do not change form whatever the tense may be.

Example: hurt, born, cut, hit

Match the present tense and past tense verbs.

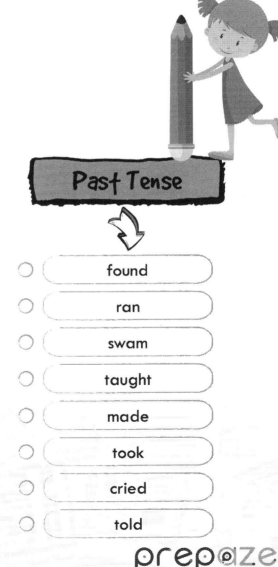

Conjugate

Complete the sentences with the irregular forms of the verbs given in the parentheses.

1. We _____ (eat) pizza for dinner.

2. I _____ (see) a bear in the woods.

3. The children _____ (sing) the national anthem.

4. Please _____ (shut) the door after you.

5. Tony _____ (buy) a blue car.

6. The people _____ (rise) when the flag was hoisted.

7. Last night, my sister _____ (hear) a noise outside her window.

8. My aunt _____ (set) the table for Thanksgiving lunch.

9. Nana _____ (spread) butter on my toast.

10. I _____ (know) she would get angry.

 Did You Know?

Adding an "s" to a noun makes it plural, whereas adding an "s" to a verb makes it singular.

Singular Noun	Plural Noun
friend	friends
Singular Verb	**Plural Verb**
sings	sing

Adjectives

Words that describe the quality of people, places, animals, or things are called adjectives.

Examples

| small | dark | dull | colorful |
| bright | spicy | loud | happy |

The given table lists adjectives. Fill in the most appropriate adjective for each word in the balloon.

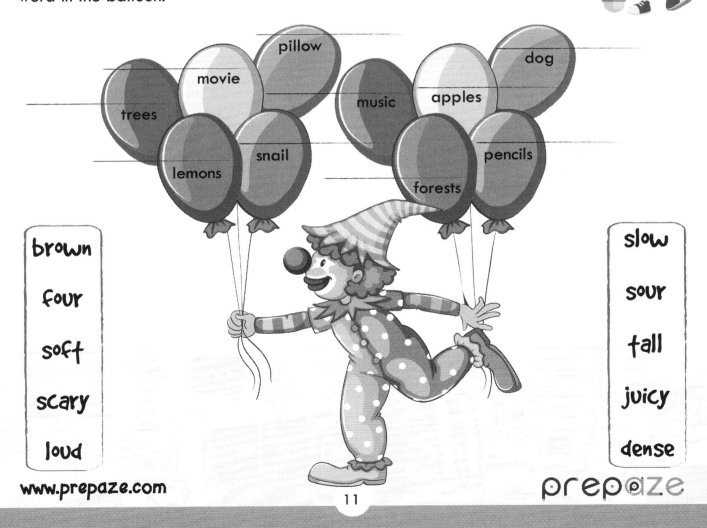

Spot the Adjectives

Read the sentences and circle the adjectives.

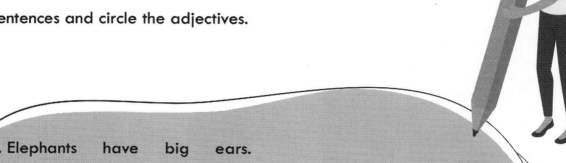

1. Elephants have big ears.

2. The coffee was bitter.

3. Porcupines have prickly quills.

4. We chose to play in the oval park.

5. When the teacher entered, the classroom was noisy.

6. This is a sharp knife.

7. The baby has blue eyes.

8. There was a mild earthquake this morning.

9. It was a thoughtful gift.

10. Andrea was happy with her scores.

Fill in the Blanks

| largest | colorful | messy | heavy | grey |
| six | black | healthy | millions | warm |

1. Sheila brought a _____ snack.

2. She bought a _____ car.

 3. I had to carry the _____ box.

4. It was a _____ day in spring.

5. My father cleaned up the _____ garage.

 6. The anaconda is the _____ snake in the world.

7. Alex ate _____ slices of the pizza.

 8. The _____ cat climbed up the tree.

9. There are _____ of stars in the universe.

 10. The child was playing with a _____ ball.

Sensory Words

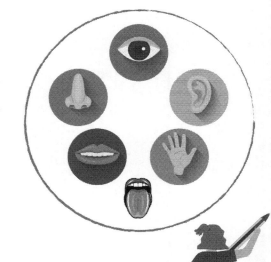

We feel the world around us with the help of our sense organs. Our sense organs help us see, smell, hear, taste, and feel things around us. Each of these senses can be described with the help of adjectives. Let us look at some of these adjectives.

Each food item shown below has a unique taste. Write the most appropriate adjective that describes it. The words can be used more than once.

| sweet | buttery | fizzy | bitter | crunchy |
| flaky | spicy | juicy | salty | creamy |

www.prepaze.com

Write down the best word from the table that describes each of them.

| cold | rough | sharp | silky | hot |
| prickly | soft | sticky | hard | smooth |

1. I could not hold the ice cube because it was _____.

2. The skin of a pineapple is _____.

3. I wore mittens as the pan was _____.

4. One side of the sandpaper is _____.

5. Ben plays with his _____ teddy bear.

6. Please draw with a _____ pencil.

7. I love that _____ scarf.

8. My fingers were _____ after I dipped them in sugar syrup.

9. The marbles were _____, so they rolled over the table.

10. The cake became _____ because the oven was too hot.

Like the sense of smell and touch, the noises you hear also have adjectives.
Read the sentences and fill in the blanks with correct words from the box.

silent

squeaky

faint

shrill

creaky

deafening

1. I could not sleep because the windows were _____

2. The thunderbolt was _____.

3. The students fell _____ when the teacher scolded them.

4. I could hear the _____ sound of the church bells from miles away.

5. The _____ ringtone of her cell phone made me jump.

6. The _____ mouse gave away its hideout.

The sense of smell is just as important. Guess the adjective that describes the smell of the picture best.

| delicious | smoky | stinky |
| stale | rotten | fresh |

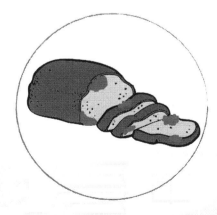

Adverbs

Words that describe how an action happens are called adverbs. They also describe, where, when, or how often an action happens.

Examples

How? quickly, brightly, happily
When? now, then, tomorrow, never, always, sometimes
Where? inside, outside, here, there, up, down

Underline the adverbs in each sentence.

1. The tortoise trundled along slowly.

2. The hare ran faster than the tortoise.

3. I went inside to get my umbrella.

4. The mailman carried the package carefully to the car.

5. Nina slept peacefully.

6. The dog barked loudly at the mailman.

7. Mike and Sam have always been best friends.

8. It snowed heavily during Christmas.

9. Ben quietly walked behind mother.

10. The kitten purred happily.

Circle the Adverbs

tiny   purple   five
soon   near
playfully   quietly   hopefully
honestly   crooked   hungry
shiny

Adjective or Adverb?

Rewrite the sentences by changing the wrong adjective or adverb.

1. You must read the instructions careful.

_____

2. When I saw him last, he was sitting comfortable in the chair.

_____

3. The loudly noise woke me up.

_____

4. Dan quiet entered the room.

_____

5. That man is wearing smell socks.

_____

6. The calmly people waited in line.

_____

7. My uncle bought me a deliciously candy.

_____

8. Mr. Connors drove us to the park in his newly car.

_____

Add adjectives and adverbs to these sentences to make them more informative and interesting. One is done for you.

He ate a sandwich.	He ate a **club** sandwich.
I have a dog.	
Bobby ran.	
They are going today.	
Nick and Mona are playing.	

Capitalization

Capitalization is writing the first letter of a word in uppercase and the remaining letters in lowercase.

Rules	Examples
The first letter of the first word of a sentence is always capitalized.	**S**chool reopens next week. **L**et us watch a movie.
Proper nouns are capitalized, no matter where they occur in a sentence.	My best friend is **M**ichelle. He moved from **C**hicago. We met him after **E**aster. I met **S**enator **I**wing yesterday.
The pronoun I is always capitalized	Andy and **I** went to the ball game.

Choose the best answer.

1. _____ visited the zoo.
   a. My friends and i
   b. My friends and I
   c. my friends and I
   d. my friends and i

3. Nancy went to high school at _____.
   a. San Jose
   b. San jose
   c. san Jose
   d. san jose

2. _____ is the highest peak in the world.
   a. Mount Everest
   b. Mount everest
   c. mount Everest
   d. mount everest

4. _____ was the sixteenth president of the United states of America.
   a. Abraham Lincoln
   b. abraham Lincoln
   c. Abraham lincoln
   d. abraham lincoln

5. The dentist asked _____ to visit her on _____.
   a. me, tuesday
   b. Me, Tuesday
   c. me, Tuesday
   d. Me, tuesday

Rewrite the sentences applying capitalization rules.

1. jane, tina, and i are going out to play.

_____

_____

2. dr. tucker said we could visit him on monday.

_____

_____

3. elaine's family is going to disneyland for spring break.

_____

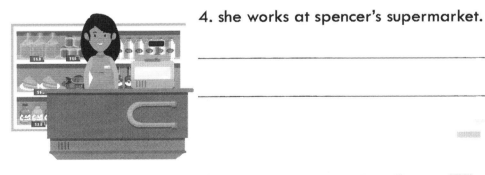

4. she works at spencer's supermarket.

_____

_____

5. i saw ron walk past.

_____

Commas

A **comma** is a punctuation mark that provides a pause to separate words, clauses, or ideas within a sentence. They are used to provide clarity.

Rules	Examples
Commas are used to separate words in a series.	Dogs, cats, and turtles are pets.
They are used to separate introductory phrases.	With some help, you can finish this faster.
They are used before or after quotation marks.	I said, "Please stay!" "Don't you dare!", he cried.

Add commas where necessary.

1. I had soup a sandwich and a cake.

2. If we leave now we can reach on time.

3. Mark said "I am glad you could come!"

4. I told her but she forgot.

5. Yes it is her watch.

Apostrophes

Apostrophes are used to form possessives or to form contractions.

Rules	Examples
Used to answer the question "whose?"	This is **Tony's** bike. These are my **grandfather's** books.
Used while mentioning the last two digits of the year (date).	Rock and Roll became popular in the **'40s**. (years 1940 to 1949.)
Used for contractions (to combine words).	I **don't** know. (do + not) They'd left. (They + had)

Add Apostrophes

The following sentences lack apostrophes. Add apostrophes wherever necessary.

1. Hes been sick for a week now.

2. This is someone elses bag.

3. Whys the dog barking?

4. I have borrowed Garys watch.

5. The movie, The Lion King, was released in 94.

Contractions

Write down the contractions of the words using apostrophes.

Words	Contractions
I would	
I am	
you are	
are not	
It is	
Let us	

Read the passage and add commas and apostrophes where necessary.

One foggy morning Jane and Ken went out for a walk with Kens dog Buddy. As

they walked slowly Buddy scampered ahead. Jane spotted a

mushroom and said "This is an ants umbrella!".

Ken looked at the dewdrops on the leaves and said "This is the

ladybugs water cooler!". Right then Buddy picked up a bone and barked "Woof! This

is a lucky dogs breakfast!"

Spelling Patterns

Spelling words correctly is an important part of knowing to read and write English. For the most part, the letters have a pattern in which they are spelled.

Examples

There are many patterns. For example, soft C is when "c" represents "s" sound in words such as:

city, dance, bicycle

Read the paragraph given below and write down the words that have **ir, er, ur,** and **ear**. Say the words aloud and find out how they are similar.

Hi! I am Chester. My twin sister Jennifer and I are in third grade at Jefferson Elementary School. We have blond, curly hair. Our birthday falls on the thirteenth of December every year. Last year, Aunt Esther gifted her a purple skirt and me a furry jacket. We like to celebrate our birthday together.

Words with er	Words with ir	Words with ur	Words with ear

Read the paragraph given below and write down the words that have **oy, oi**. Say the words aloud and find out how they are similar.

Joyce has joined her school basketball team. She comes home late after practice. Her mom covers her dinner in tinfoil and leaves it in the oven, so it won't get spoiled. She also boils some soy milk and leaves it on the table. Joyce enjoys this dinner. She records the points she has scored during practice on the white board in the foyer. She takes a picture of this and sends it to the boys and girls in her class. Sometimes, when her joints ache, she gets the royal treatment of breakfast in bed!

Words with oy	Words with oi

Here are some words related to Easter. Circle the correct spellings.

- Happy
- Happi
- Happie

- Candi
- Candy
- Cendi

- Bunny
- Bunnie
- Bunni

- Aags
- Eggs
- Eags

- Beskit
- Baskit
- Basket

- Sonday
- Sondai
- Sunday

This or That?

Choose the correct spelling.

1. Be _____ to each other. (nice/nise)

2. My _____ is close by. (houce/house)

3. The fox jumped _____ the fence. (over/ower)

4. The _____ is full of books. (bocks/box)

5. The _____ to draw water from the well is very old. (roap/rope)

6. There was a strange _____ at my window. (bird/burd)

7. Get _____ my bike. (of/off)

8. She is wearing a new _____ . (coat/cote)

9. It might _____ today. (snoe/snow)

10. We put up our _____ at 9 'O clock. (tant/tent)

English is tricky! Learn your spellings and have a good time writing!

Context Clues

When we read something new, more often than not, we come across words we do not know. They may be hard to spell but not always do we have a dictionary handy. How do we then make out the meanings of these words?

The first thing to do is to circle or underline the unknown word. Then look at the surrounding words for clues.

Example

> My mother cooks better than the **caterers** who brought food for the party.

Though the word "caterers" may be new to some of us, we can guess the meaning of the word using the clues in the surrounding. The words "cooks" and "food" help us understand that caterers are people who provide food and drink for an event.

This or That?

Each sentence has an underlined word. Two words are provided on either side of the sentence. Circle one word which has the same meaning as the underlined word.

boxed	She penned a letter to her father.	wrote
rich	The charity event was hosted for the wealthy for donations.	handy-men
naughty	The cruel boy threw out his brother's homework.	mean
hot	Abdul could not walk in the sweltering desert.	raining
looked at	Mike nibbled on the toast.	ate slowly
wanting to know	The curious kitten jumped off the wall.	feeling better
built on	The blocks toppled over.	fell over
write again	My teacher made me repeat the lines.	say again
make ready	Sophie has to prepare dinner.	cut fruits
drinks medicine	Uncle Sam dozes off quickly.	sleeps

Understand the context and complete the sentences with the most appropriate word from the table.

leash

various

beneath

witty

immense

glimmered

beverages

aroma

perched

glared

1. The student gave a _____ answer to the teacher.

2. They offered _____ like milk, tea, and coffee.

3. The dog ran when he was let off the _____.

4. When Amy answered back, her mother _____ at her.

5. The _____ of spaghetti made my mouth water.

6. The florist sells _____ flowers in summer.

7. Michael Jordan has an _____ fan base.

8. The mouse was caught _____ a block of wood.

9. The crow was _____ on the tree.

10. The fireflies _____ in the far away fields.

Use the Context

Find the meaning of the underlined words. Write down what you think the meaning of the word is.

1. Cindy was excited to be the first to go on the stage. She was <u>trembling</u> a little as this was her first competition.

_____

2. Dad gave us a choice of <u>beverage</u>. He had lemonade, milk, and orange juice set out on the table.

_____

3. The difference between two numbers is found by <u>subtraction</u>.

_____

4. Dinosaurs became <u>extinct</u> about sixty five million years ago.

_____

5. When winter <u>approaches</u>, mules move down to the foothills to warmer weather.

_____

Root Words

A root word is the smallest form of a word, before anything is added to it. A prefix or a suffix may be added to the word, with or without changing the meaning of the word.

Example

the root word in **talking** is **talk**. **ing** is added to it to change its tense.

Write down the root word of every word underlined.

Sentence	Root word	
Mary said Tom is **friendly.**		
The bird was **hopping** on the path.		
We can reach Florida **faster** by plane.		
Joey has nothing to be **ashamed** of.		
The boy felt **sleepy** after having the medicine.		
I am very **thankful** to Ann for helping me.		
The fog began to **disappear**.		
My **teacher** is the best of them all.		
The **speaker** was the mayor of the town.		

www.prepaze.com

For the root word given in the parentheses, add prefixes/suffixes and fill in the blanks.

1. I am _____ (luck) to have you as my sister.

2. Due to flu, Sam is _____ (able) to go to the party.

3. We have an _____ (enjoy) time when Uncle Bobby visits.

4. That was the _____ (smart) move I could have made.

5. This answer is _____ (correct) please redo.

Compound Words

When two words together give a new meaning, the new word is called a compound word.

Example

The word **homework** uses two words **home** and **work**.

Similarly **bathrobe** uses two words **bath** and **robe**.

Form compound words with the help of the pictures given.

pan +	(cake)		(cake)
butter +	(fly)		(butterfly)
news +	(paper)		(newspaper)
water +	(fall)		(fall)
cart +	(wheel)		(wheel)
cross +	(walk)		(walk)
star +	(fish)		(fish)
bath +	(tub)		(tub)
sun +	(flower)		(flower)
lunch +	(box)		(box)

Underline the compound words used in each sentence.

1. The mailman was on time.

2. The rainbow has seven colors.

3. Rex plays basketball every other day.

4. This is Easter Sunday.

5. She added mint to watermelon juice.

6. The warm sunshine woke me up this morning.

7. The first snowfall of the year is always beautiful.

8. Aunt Tanya put the wrong key in the keyhole.

9. I turned on the flashlight when the power went out.

10. Mom bought everything that was on the list.

Shades of Meanings

Think of the color blue. Now, which blue came to your mind? Light blue? Dark blue? Just like colors have shades, verbs and adjectives have shades too! The shades convey the intensity of the words.

Example

The adjectives **big, huge,** and **gigantic** all mean big, but they differ in intensity.

Arrange each set of words in the order of strength. The strongest being on the top of the list.

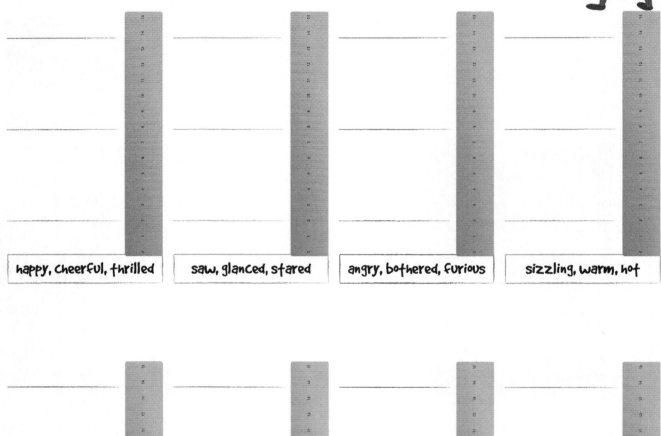

Reading: Literature

Unity Is Strength

Read the story about unity, which means being together, and answer the questions that follow.

Once upon a time, a flock of pigeons flew in search of food. They came across grains scattered[1] in the shade of a banyan tree. The hungry pigeons swooped down and began to eat.

They did not see the net that was spread by the hunter under the grains. Soon they were all trapped in the net. The pigeons were scared and fluttered their wings helplessly trying to get out, but could not.

Then, the leader of the flock had an idea. He asked the pigeons to fly up together carrying the net with them.

They flew to a nearby village. In the village, lived a mouse who was their friend. They knew he could help them. When the mouse saw them land with the net, he bravely got into action and started chewing on the net with his teeth. Soon all the birds were set free.

They were very happy and thanked the mouse for help. They then flew away together into the evening sky.

When we work together, we can face challenges and come out successful.

[1]**scattered**: spread over an area

Missing Letters

Complete the words.

1. What were the pigeons flying in search of?	f __ __ d
2. Where did the pigeons find the grains?	under a b __ __ __ __ n tree
3. Who had spread the net to trap the pigeons?	the h __ __ __ __ r
4. Why did the pigeons fly looking for the mouse?	for h __ __ p
5. How did the mouse set the pigeons free?	c __ __ __ __ d on the net

What Is the Feeling?

Match the pigeons' feelings to the action.

- hungry ○   ○ flew together carrying the net
- scared ○   ○ thanked the mouse for setting them free
- brave   ○   ○ swooped down to eat the grains
- happy   ○   ○ fluttered their wings to get out of the net

www.prepaze.com

Jumbled Sentences

Sequence the sentences in the correct order

	The pigeons decided to fly away with the net.
	The mouse chewed the net and set them free.
	They swooped down to eat the grains.
	They thanked the mouse and flew away together.
	They flew to a village to find their friend, a mouse.
	A flock of hungry pigeons saw some grains scattered under the banyan tree.
	They were trapped in the net spread by a hunter.

What do you think would have happened if....

(Tick the answer you find most appropriate.)

1. the pigeons had noticed the net before swooping down?

a. They would not have been trapped in the net.

b. They would have been trapped in the net.

2. the pigeons had been fluttering their wings helplessly without thinking?

a. The hunter would have caged them.

b. The hunter would have set them free.

3. the mouse was not in the village to see them land?

a. The pigeons would have been disappointed.

b. They would have found another way to set themselves free.

A Visit to the Farmhouse

Spring came early this year. The cousins, Frankie, Bony, Bobby, Timmy, and Joey did not have to wait until April for the **onset** of spring. They were already **excited**.

Aunt Mona had invited them to her farmhouse for Easter. The cousins loved visiting the farm.

On the day they **arrived** at the farm, Aunt Mona was ready with the **schedule** for Easter egg hunt.

Joey was the naughtiest of the cousins. During an **outdoor** egg hunt, he climbed the roof of the stable. The roof was old. One tile **collapsed**, sending Joey down into a stack of hay. A huge tub landed on him too! Joey called out to his cousins, but no one could hear him.

Hearing his cries, the horses understood he was in **trouble**. They kicked the stacks of hay and pushed the tub away. They pulled Joey out by the sleeve of his shirt.

By this time the cousins came looking for Joey.

When the cousins **narrated** the story to Aunt Mona, she was glad that he **escaped** unhurt!

Story Elements

1. Who are the characters in the passage?
_____

2. Who was the naughtiest among them?
_____

3. What are the cousins excited about?
_____

4. What activity was planned for them at their arrival at the farmhouse?
_____

5. What happened to Joey?
_____

6. Who helped Joey when he was in trouble?
_____

7. How did Aunt Mona react when she heard what happened?
_____

Guess the Meaning

Choose the closest meaning of the words printed in bold font in the context of the passage.

onset
- a) beginning
- b) ending
- c) setting up

excited
- a) going out
- b) spotting
- c) thrilled

schedule
- a) travel plan
- b) plan
- c) hunting

outdoor
- a) outside
- b) gate
- c) open the door

collapsed
- a) together
- b) fell
- c) dead

trouble
- a) two
- b) rubbish
- c) difficulty

narrated
- a) told
- b) enacted
- c) hid from

escaped
- a) plan
- b) set free
- c) fell down

Mother Earth

Look at the garbage around you,

In the land and water too!

If you don't do something about it soon,

Other living beings will cry and swoon!

They'd say, "Slow down humans! We want our space.

Earth is also our homebase[1]!"

Take good care of what Mother Earth gives you,

She will give you more and that is true!

---

[1] **homebase:** the place where someone or something operates from.

Poem Appreciation

1. Which word means rubbish or waste?
   _____
   _____

2. Which word means faint?
   _____
   _____

3. Which word means a place where someone lives?
   _____
   _____

4. Who are the "other" living beings here?
   _____
   _____

5. The poet says "She will give you more." What does this mean?
   _____
   _____

6. What is the poet trying to convey in this poem?
   _____
   _____
   _____

The Rainbow

Spring had just set in. With flowers blooming and the leaves sprouting[1] on trees, I was ready to go out to walk Rocco, my dog.

It was drizzling when we stepped out. Rocco and I decided to make it quick and be back before it started raining. We had just walked ten yards from home when it started pouring. We ran back indoors.

Rocco, lay at my feet, whimpering and whining occasionally[2]. I told Rocco that I was just as disappointed as he was. Just after an hour, it stopped raining and the sun peeked through the clouds.

Rocco and I bolted out the door. The air seemed cleaner. The smell of rain on fresh grass was pleasant. Just as we walked half a mile, I spotted a beautiful rainbow on the horizon.

Standing there, with Rocco, I took in the beauty of the colorful arch on the sky and I told myself, "Totally worth the wait!"

Read and Answer

1. Who is referred to as "I" throughout the passage?

    a) the dog

    b) the boy

    c) the author

2. What is the point of view used by the narrator?

    a) first person

    b) second person

    c) third person

---

[1] **sprouting:** start to grow
[2] **occasionally:** not often, but sometimes

3. When did the events in the passage take place?

   a) in summer

   b) in winter

   c) in spring

4. What did the narrator and the dog do when it started to rain?

   a) They took shelter under a tree.

   b) They ran back home.

   c) They continued walking in rain.

5. Why were the dog and the narrator disappointed?

   a) They were not able to see a rainbow due to rain.

   b) They were hungry from walking too long.

   c) They were not able to complete their walk due to rain.

6. Where did they spot the rainbow?

   a) on the grass

   b) on the horizon

   c) on the door

7. How did the narrator feel in the end?

   a) elated

   b) terrified

   c) anxious

8. What is the meaning of disappointed as used in the passage?

   a) angry

   b) unhappy

   c) satisfied

9. Which of the words from the passage means enjoyable?

   a) whimpering

   b) peeked

   c) pleasant

10. What is the author's purpose in writing this passage?

    a) to entertain us by sharing an experience

    b) to persuade us by asking us to take walks every day

    c) to explain how rainbows are formed

Story Analysis

Read the given narrative and identify the introduction, sequence of events, and conclusion. Complete the template below.

Narrative

Topic:

Title:

Catchy first sentence:

| Event 1 | Event 2 | Event 3 |

Last sentence:

Reading: Informational Text

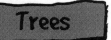

Trees are the most valuable parts of our surroundings.

Have you ever looked for the shade of a tree on a hot day?

Trees not only give us shade, but many other things. They give us food such as nuts and fruit.

Wood from trees is used to build houses and make furniture.

Trees are home to many animals such as birds, squirrels, and lizards.

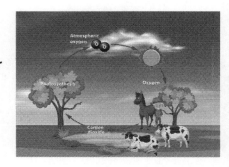

But most importantly, trees help keep living things alive. They take in the carbon dioxide that we breathe out and fill the air with oxygen for us to breathe in!

Trees are a boon to all living things. So, they should not be cut down. Wouldn't you agree?

Read and Answer

1. What is the main purpose of this passage?

   a) to persuade

   b) to educate

   c) to entertain

2. Which is the word most frequently used in the passage?

   a) parts

   b) you

   c) tree

3. Who uses trees as homes?

   a) birds and lizards

   b) squirrels

   c) both a and b

4. Which of the following statements is true?

   a) The only use of trees is to make furniture.

   b) Trees give us shade and oxygen.

   c) No other animal can live in trees besides birds.

5. Which of the following statements is false?

   a) Trees are an essential part of our surroundings.

   b) Trees help keep living things alive.

   c) Trees fill the air with carbon dioxide.

In the table, list two key details and reasons that support the author's view in the passage. One is done for you.

Important Point	Key Detail	Reasons/Evidences
Trees are a boon to all living things.	Trees are home to animals.	birds, squirrels, and lizards
1.		
2.		

Cats or Dogs

Here are two passages giving information about cats and dogs. Read the passages and make a decision whether you would like a cat or a dog for a pet!

Cats as Pets

Cats are great pets for children. They are a joy to be around. They cuddle up and make purring noises when they are petted.

Cats are easy to take care of; they don't need to be bathed. They lick themselves clean.

Cats don't need to be walked outside either. They use litter boxes which can be placed inside the house. These boxes need to be cleaned regularly, though.

Cats have a sharp hearing capacity. They can hear a mouse in a hole, while humans can't.

Cats also sleep a lot - about eighteen hours a day! So they hardly bother people while they do their chores.

Dogs as Pets

Dogs make wonderful pets. They are happy and cheerful animals.

Dogs show their feelings with their tails. They are cuddly and like to be petted.

Dogs like to be outdoors. Most dogs hate a bath, but it is important for their cleanliness.

Dogs have sensitive[1] noses. They can sniff out rats, insects or strangers around the house.

Dogs are always alert[2]. They are light sleepers and cock up their ears for sounds, even while sleeping. Even if they do fall asleep, they are ready to go the moment they are woken!

---

[1] **sensitive:** quick to respond
[2] **alert:** quick to see

Understanding Text

1. What is the author's purpose in writing these passages?

   a) to help the readers understand which pet is suitable for them

   b) to enlighten the readers that cats and dogs can live together

   c) to prove that dogs are a better pet than cats

2. According to the passages, it is easier to take care of which pet?

   a) cats

   b) dogs

   c) both cats and dogs

3. What is the point of view used in both the passages?

   a) first person

   b) second person

   c) third person

4. Which of these can a cat do that a human cannot according to the passage?

   a) clean themselves

   b) walk themselves

   c) hear a mouse in a hole

5. What do most dogs dislike?

   a) being petted

   b) being given a bath

   c) being taken for a walk

Compare and Contrast

Sometimes it is necessary to make decisions such as which tree to plant in the backyard or which car to buy. At such times, it helps to read up on topics and get as much information as possible before making a decision. One author's view may be totally different from another's. What do you do? You will have to sift through and find the similarities and differences in their opinions and make a decision based on what will suit you best.

Fill in the important points, key details, and reasons in the table comparing the passages on cats and dogs.

	Title	Important Point	Key Detail	Reasons/Evidences
Passage 1				
Passage 2				

Go through the table you just filled out and write down the similarities and differences between the information given in the two passages.

Compare and Contrast
&

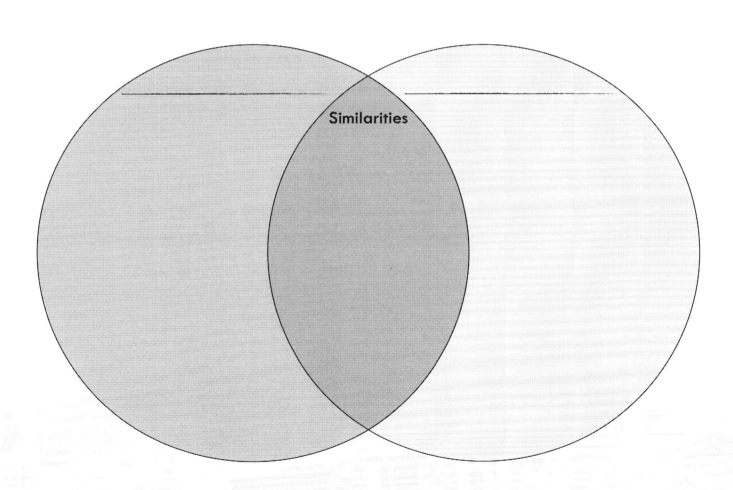

Pizza

Pizza is a dish from Italy. It is a flat bread with a variety of toppings. The crust of a pizza can be regular, deep-dish, or thin crust.

I like deep-dish pizza because it has lots of cheese, and I get to pick what I want as toppings. Some days I choose vegetables and some days I choose meat. I can make my pizza as spicy as I want it to be. Even the thought of Jalapeño Popper Pizzas can make my mouth water!

With a crust that can be as thin or thick as one wants, and the choice of toppings, and spices to make it taste the way one likes it, pizzas do make a great meal, anytime of the day. Don't you agree?

Read and Answer

1. According to the passage, which is a dish from Italy?

    a) bread

    b) pizza

    c) cheese

2. How many types of crusts are mentioned in the passage?

    a) two

    b) three

    c) four

3. What is the author's purpose in writing this passage?

    a) to persuade us to choose deep-dish pizza always

    b) to educate us about the origin of pizza

    c) to share his or her opinion on preferred pizza

4. Which of these reasons are valid to show why the author likes deep dish pizza?

    a) The author prefers it as it is a dish from Italy.

    b) The author prefers it as it has toppings of his/her choice.

    c) The author prefers it as it can be had anytime of the day.

5. Who is referred to as "you" in the passage?

    a) the author

    b) the audience

    c) the Italians

Fact or Opinion

A fact is something which can be proven true.

For example: The sky is blue.

The sky is blue for everyone. It does not change for each person.

An opinion, on the other hand, is what you think or how you feel about something.

An opinion can differ from one person to another.

For example:

Wionna: I love salads because they are good for health.

Arnold: "I don't like salads because they have vegetables."

Read the given passage. With the help of the steps mentioned earlier, identify the topic, opinion, reasons and conclusion and fill in the given template.

Opinion

Topic: ....

Opinion:
....
....

Reason 1	Reason 2	Reason 3

Conclusion:
....
....

Color the Balloons

Read the sentence in each balloon. If it is an opinion, color the balloon grey. If it is a fact, color the balloon black.

- Insects are creepy.
- Pear is a fruit.
- Rugby is a sport.
- Pumpkin pie is tastier than apple pie.
- Disney World is in Florida.
- It is fun to play in the rain.
- The month of August comes after July.
- Going to school on Saturday is funny.

For each word frame a sentence which states a fact and one that states an opinion.

Word	Fact	Opinion
chips		
roses		
chocolate		
parrot		
music		

Life Cycle of a Hen

A hen lays an egg almost once in twenty-five hours. She sits on the eggs for three weeks, keeping them warm all the time.

At the end of the three-week period, little chicks hatch out. It takes about three months for these chicks to grow into adult chicken.

When they are about a year old, they are known as hens.

When you read the passage did you also look at the picture alongside? This picture is known as a diagram or an illustration.

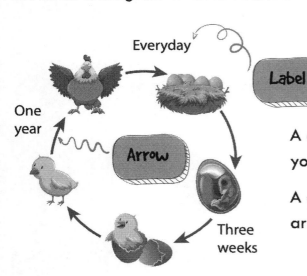

The stages in the life cycle of a hen

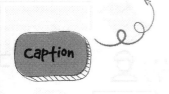

A diagram is a picture, plan or a chart that helps you understand the text better.

A diagram usually has photographs, drawings, arrows, labels, and captions.

Each of these features is important. Here, the arrows show the order of the stages of development, the labels mention the stage and the caption describes what the diagram is about.

Understanding Text

1. In how many days does an egg hatch?

    a) 24 hours

    b) 3 weeks

    c) 3 months

2. Why does a hen sit on its eggs?

    a) to warm the eggs and keep the temperature in the proper range

    b) to break the eggs and help the chicks come out of the eggs

    c) to multiply the eggs and make more chicks

3. How many days does it take a chick to grow into an adult chicken?

    a) 24 hours

    b) 3 weeks

    c) 3 months

4. When do the chicks become a hen?

    a) after three weeks

    b) after three months

    c) after a year

5. According to the illustration, how many stages are there in the life cycle of a hen?

    a) three stages

    b) four stages

    c) five stages

6. What is an illustration?

    a) a diagram to support the text

    b) a picture to understand the text

    c) both a and b

Study the Illustration

Use the picture on the right and the words given in the box to complete the sentences below.

Photosynthesis

| oxygen | Sugar | water | carbon dioxide | sunlight |

In order to make their own food, green plants use _____

from the sun and _____ from the soil. They also use the

_____ from the air.

In this process, _____ is formed on the leaves. The plants

give out _____

Reading: Foundational Skills

Long and Short Vowels

Vowels and consonants: The alphabet is made of 26 letters. Of these the letters **a, e, i, o,** and **u** are called vowels and the rest are known as consonants.

Vowels are letters that, when called out, produce a sound that is not blocked by the mouth or throat.

Example

Read out these vowels and consonants and see the difference.

a	b	e	f	i	g	o	z	u
x	i	j	y	m	u	p	a	e

There is one special letter of the alphabet, **y**, which sometimes functions as a consonant and sometimes as a vowel.

It is consonant when it appears as the first letter of a word.
Example: yard, yam

When it appears elsewhere in the word, it functions as a vowel.
Example: sky, merry

Spot the Vowels

Underline the vowel in the following words

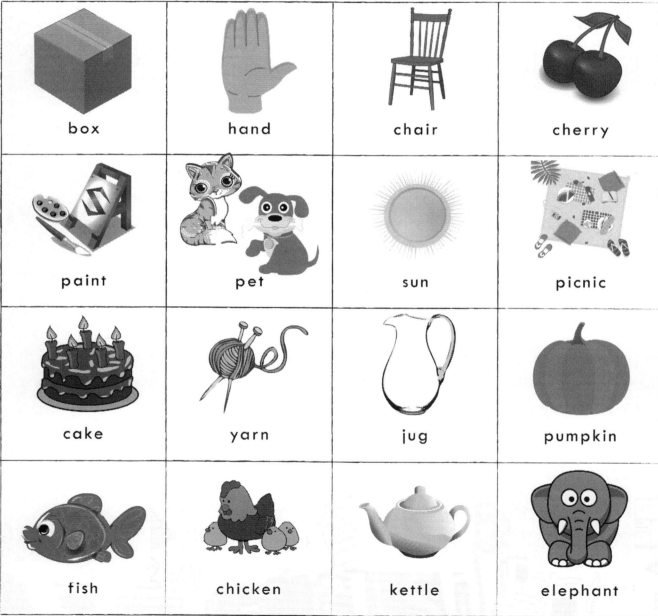

box	hand	chair	cherry
paint	pet	sun	picnic
cake	yarn	jug	pumpkin
fish	chicken	kettle	elephant

Vowels have two types of sounds: short vowel and long vowel.

Short vowels usually sound softer and relaxed.

Spelling and Sound

Read out each word given below. Pay attention to the sound of the vowels in these words. These are short vowel sounds. Write down one word that contains a short vowel.

a		cat	------
e		bell	------
i		fish	------
o		dog	------
u		bus	------

Long vowels usually sound like they are pronounced or sometimes lengthier.

Readout each word given below. Pay attention to the sound of the vowels in these words. These are long vowel sounds. Write down one word that contains the long vowel.

a		apple	
e		tree	
i		light	
o		bow	
u		tune	

Compare the sounds of each short and long vowel and pay attention to the difference in sound.

www.prepaze.com

Read out what each picture shows and circle the word.

☁❄	slow	snow	show
⛵	barn	bow	boat
📌	pin	pen	pan
⬭	over	oven	oval
🌹	rise	rose	row

Long vowel *a* may sound like the letter **a** or the sound of **ai** as in "chain," or **ay** as in "bay."

Use **a, ai,** or **ay** to spell the word given in the picture.

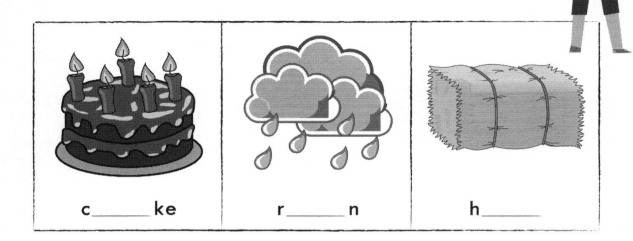

c____ke   r____n   h____

Long vowel **e** sounds like the vowel itself, but takes on different spellings in words. **For example:** ea in beach, ey in money and ee in free.

Use **ea, ey,** or **ee** to spell the word given in the picture.

p____s   thr____   hon____

Long vowel **i** sounds like the vowel itself, but just like the vowel **e**, it also takes on different spellings.

For example: igh in tight and **ie** in lie.

Use **i**, **igh**, or **ie** to spell the word given in the picture.

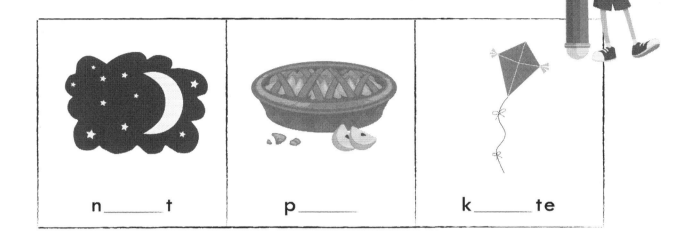

n_____t   p_____   k_____te

Long vowel **o** sounds like the vowel itself, but just like the vowels **e** and **i**, it also takes on different spellings.

For example: oa in boat and **ow** in row.

Use **o**, **oa**, or **ow** to spell the word given in the picture.

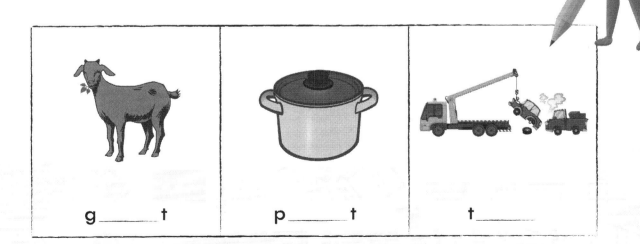

g_____t   p_____t   t_____

Long vowel **u** sounds like the vowel itself, but just like the vowels **i** and **o**, it also takes on different spellings.

For example: **ue** in true, **oo** in soon, and **ou** in mouth.

Use **u**, **ue**, **oo**, or **ou** to spell the word given in the picture.

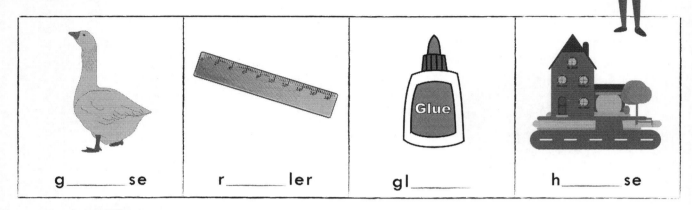

g____se   r____ler   gl____   h____se

Now that you have learned the long vowel sounds, identify as many long vowel words in the table of letters given.

Missing Vowels

Fill in the blanks.

1	A cl __ __ n came to my birthday party.	
2	I drank hot s __ __ p.	
3	Please save a s __ __ t for me.	
4	Jerry is a m __ __ se.	
5	My father will m __ __ the lawn this Sunday.	
6	Shall we go to the b __ __ ch this evening?	
7	A kangaroo carries its baby in the p __ __ ch.	
8	I have to wash my f __ __ t before I go to bed.	
9	The monk __ __ was sitting on the branch.	
10	Let me get my c __ __ t.	

www.prepaze.com

Two-Syllable Words

When a word contains two vowel sounds, it is said to have two syllables.

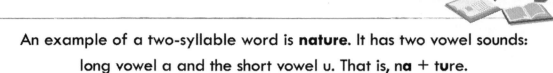

Example

An example of a two-syllable word is **nature**. It has two vowel sounds: long vowel a and the short vowel u. That is, n**a** + t**u**re.

Similarly, the word **over** is a two-syllable word with two vowel sounds, long vowel and short vowel e. That is, **o** + **ver**.

On either side of the word, write the two syllables that make up the word.

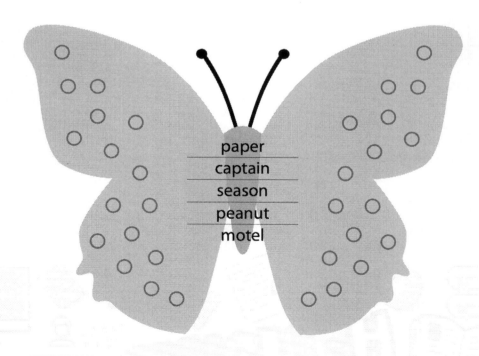

paper
captain
season
peanut
motel

As you just learned, the long and short vowels are spelled differently. Here is an activity that shows these differences in sound as well as spelling.

Fill in the correct words from the box to complete the sentence.

| write | city | ball | pretty | sky |

1. The _____ is always blue in the month of July.

2. I am going to fly to New York _____

3. The baby crawled after the _____

4. The girl was shy and _____

5. I cannot _____ on the board with a white marker.

Prefixes and Suffixes

A **prefix** is a set of letters that is added to the beginning of a word. It changes the meaning of a word.

When prefixes such as un, dis, mis are added before words they make the word negative. The prefix re is used to convey redoing or repeating something.

Examples

untidy, disrespect, mistrust, rebuild

A **suffix**, on the other hand, is a set of letters added to the end of a word. Some suffixes change a word's meaning, whereas, some change the function.

Examples

useless, joyful, waited, waiting, loudly, tallest

Draw a line to connect the appropriate prefixes and suffixes to make meaningful words.

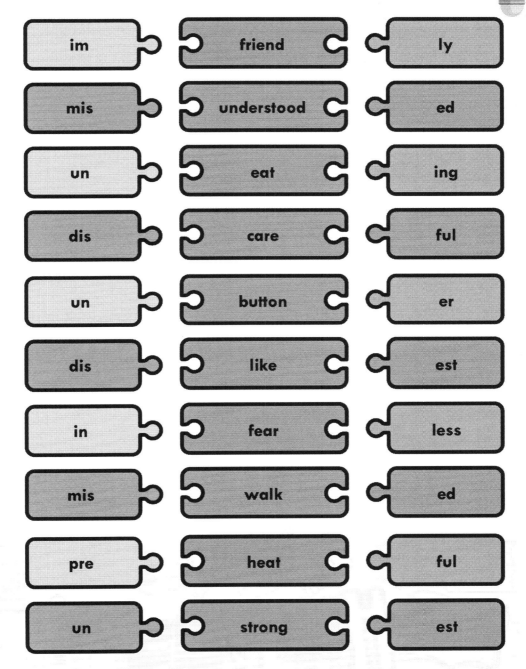

Fill in the blanks with the appropriate prefix from the table.

She was _____ able to attend the ceremony.

Lyle _____ owned the book.

Dad said, we will _____ paint the house this summer.

Grandma wears _____ focal glasses.

Some countries have a _____ color flag.

The shopkeeper has to _____ pay us for the faulty toaster.

Please _____ lock the door for me.

I bought a _____ paid calling card.

A shape with three sides is a _____ angle.

The stranger was _____ led by the locals.

We have a _____ monthly payment plan.

Help me _____ wrap the gift.

_____ cook the apples for ten minutes.

Do not _____ obey the traffic rules.

You cannot _____ use this laptop.

Write these words on a notebook and see their reflection in a mirror.

TOOT	
YAY	
OTTO	

Can you think of more such words? Use a mirror to check your work.

Writing

Opinion Writing

Writing opinion pieces is an art. It helps justify a viewpoint with reasons. There are a few steps to follow while writing opinion pieces:

1. Introduce the topic.
2. State your opinion.
3. List reasons to support your opinion.
4. Write a conclusion to sum up your opinion.

> Leo likes fish so much that he wants to have them for pets. He would like to write his opinion and ask his father for a fish tank with colorful fish.

Imagine you are Leo and write a paragraph to your father.

In the below template do the prewriting. Once you gather the points, write the paragraph in the space provided.

Opinion

Topic ....

Opinion:

Reason 1	Reason 2	Reason 3

Conclusion:

Now that planning is complete. Write your first draft here.

Fish as Pets

Explanatory Writing

Choose one of the following topics to write.

➡ How to prepare a dish

➡ How to make a project

➡ How to arrange a family gathering

In the beginning, clearly explain what all you need.

Then, describe the process in 4 to 5 steps.

Narrative Writing

Listening to stories is fun. Story-telling can be fun too! It is not just entertaining but there is always a message that is conveyed in a story. A story is one elaborate event or a sequence of events. Sometimes, the same story can be told from another perspective, or angle, by a different person.

Here are a few steps for you to follow while writing narratives:

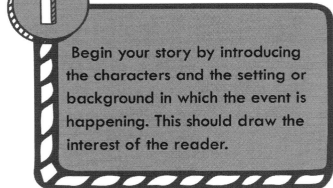

1. Begin your story by introducing the characters and the setting or background in which the event is happening. This should draw the interest of the reader.

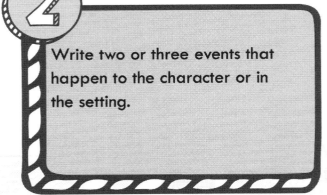

2. Write two or three events that happen to the character or in the setting.

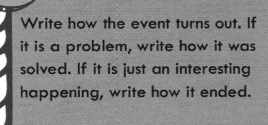

3. Write how the event turns out. If it is a problem, write how it was solved. If it is just an interesting happening, write how it ended.

4. Write how the character felt at the end.

Do you remember a scary dream you had? How did you feel when you woke up? Write a narrative by planning the introduction and sequence of events in the template.

Narrative

Topic: ....

Title: ....

Catchy first sentence:
....
....

Event 1
....
....
....

Event 2
....
....
....

Event 3
....
....
....

Last sentence:
....
....

Now that planning is complete. Write your first draft here.

A Scary Dream

Did You Know?

Every letter of the alphabet can be fit in a single sentence. Such a sentence is called a **pangram**.

Check if all the 26 letters can be found in the below sentence.

> The five boxing wizards jump quickly.

Can you make a pangram? Give it a try!

Math

Use this book to enable your children to explore numbers by solving interesting puzzles and real-life problems. Engage your children with fun, colorful activities and let them fall in love with Math.

Operations and Algebraic Thinking

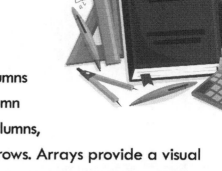

When objects, pictures, or numbers are arranged in columns and rows, the arrangement is called an **array**. Each column must contain the same number of objects as the other columns, and each row must have the same number as the other rows. Arrays provide a visual representation of the objects and help in understanding the number of objects.

Example

The following array, consisting of 4 columns and 2 rows, could be used to represent the number sentence.

Array

Number Sentences

$2 + 2 + 2 + 2 = 8$ $4 + 4 = 8$

An **even number** is a number that can be divided into two equal groups. Even numbers end in 2, 4, 6, 8, and 0.

An **odd number** is a number that cannot be divided into two equal groups. Odd numbers end in 1, 3, 5, 7, and 9.

Let's Practice

Odd and Even Numbers

1. Pair the objects to decide if the number of objects is even. Circle 'even' or 'not even' for each.

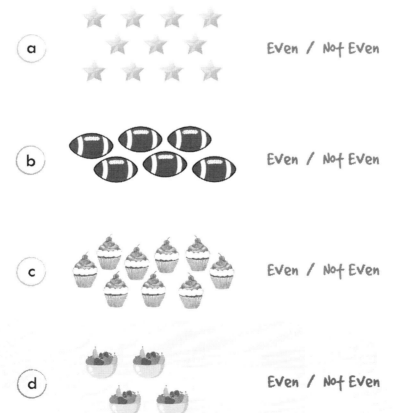

a. Even / Not Even

b. Even / Not Even

c. Even / Not Even

d. Even / Not Even

2. Solve the Word Problems.

a. Little Birdies bookstore sold 34 comic books and 12 story books. How many books did the bookstore sell in total?

b. Lisa picked 45  from the garden. She used 24 to make pasta sauce. How many tomatoes does she have left?

c. There is a 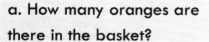 with 59 apples and 24 fewer oranges. Solve with the help of a tape diagram and number bond.

| a. How many oranges are there in the basket? | b. How many fruits are there in total? |

3. Draw to continue the pattern of the pairs in the space below until you have 5 pairs.

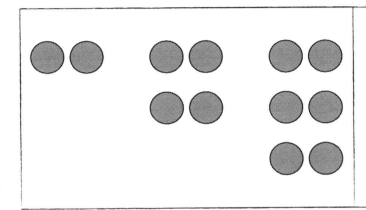

4. Circle groups of two. Count by twos to see if the number of objects is even.

There are _____ twos. There are _____ left over.

Arrays

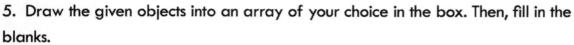 Decorate with Balloons

5. Draw the given objects into an array of your choice in the box. Then, fill in the blanks.

There are _____ rows. There are _____ columns.

There are _____ (even/odd) number of objects.

 Skip Count

6. Skip count the columns in the arrays. One has been done for you.

2

7. Draw arrays for each of these questions.

a. Circle groups of 5. Then, draw the squares into two equal rows.

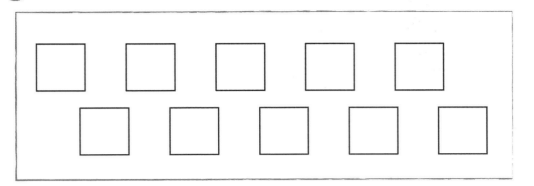

b. Circle groups of 4. Then, draw the circles into three equal columns

c. Redraw this array of hearts into rows of 2 hearts in each row.

d. Draw an array of 12 triangles.

Cupcakes and Lego Blocks

8. Complete the missing part for each.

a. Circle rows.

3 rows of _____ = _____

_____ + _____ + _____ = _____

b. Circle columns.

c. Draw an array to match 2 + 2 + 2.

5 columns of _____ = _____

_____ + _____ + _____ + _____ + _____ = _____

9. For the given array circle as given.

Circle the rows   Circle the columns

2 rows of _____ = _____   4 columns of _____ = _____

_____ + _____ = _____   _____ + _____ + _____ + _____ = _____

10. Use the array to answer each question.

a. _____ rows of _____ = 15

b. _____ columns of _____ = 15

c. _____ + _____ + _____ = _____

d. Remove 1 column. How many clouds are there?
_____

11. Draw an array with 2 rows and 3 columns and then answer the questions.

a. _____ rows of _____ = _____

b. _____ columns of _____ = _____

c. _____ + _____ + _____ = _____

12. Show two different arrays with 20 triangles.

Array 1

Array 2

13. Circle all the expressions that describe the array.

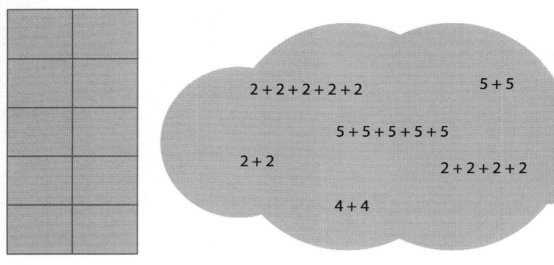

14. Solve the word problems.

a. Julie made 4 rows of 3 chairs. How many chairs did Julie use? Draw arrays and write a repeated addition number sentence to find the total.

b. Jessie's house has 2 floors with 3 windows on each floor. How many windows does his house have? Draw arrays and write a repeated addition number sentence to find the total.

c. In a card game, 3 players get 4 cards each. One more player joined the game and got the same number of cards. How many cards are dealt in total?

Draw a tape diagram and an array. Then, find the total using repeated addition.

15. Redraw the smiley faces into 2 equal groups.

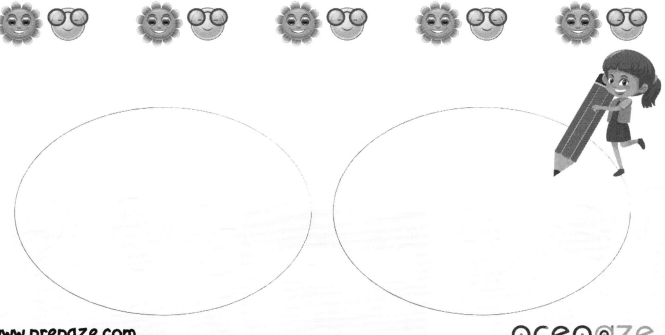

16. Jake and Ronnie solved 45 + 27 in two different ways.

Jake's work:	Ronnie's work:
45 + 27 ─── 12 60 ── 72	45 + 27 ─── 72

Explain what is different in Jake's and Ronnie's work on solving the problem

_____

_____

_____

_____

The Flower Pot Problem

17. Use the array to answer the questions.

a. _____ rows of _____ = 12

b. _____ columns of _____ = 12

c. _____ + _____ + _____ = _____

d. Add 1 more row. How many flower pots would be there?

_____

Who Won the Game?

18. Ash, Danny, and Frank are playing a game and recording their scores. For each game that they win, they get 5 points each. For every game they lose, 3 points get taken away. They all have 20 points at the start.

a. Danny won the first game. What is Danny's score?

b. Frank won the second game. What will be his score at the end of round two?

c. In the last game, Danny was the winner again. Calculate the final scores of Ash, Danny and Frank.

Ash	Danny	Frank

19. Draw an array of 'D' such that the column is 1 more than the rows. The array has 3 rows.

20. Circle the odd numbers.

21. Henry and Sam collected some stone. Henry placed them in 4 rows with 2 stones each. Sam placed them in 2 rows with 3 stones each.

a. Draw arrays to find the total stones collected by each

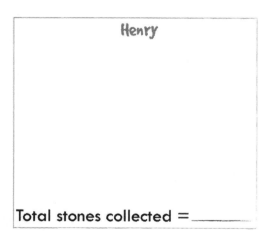

Henry	Sam
Total stones collected = _____	Total stones collected = _____

b. Who collected more stones? Color the name.

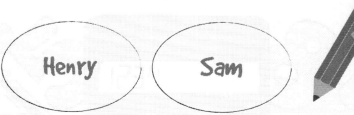

22. Add like units for the given numbers. One is done for you.

a. 76 + 23

```
   76
+  23
-----
   09
   90
   99
```

b. 23 + 32

c. 28 + 49

d. 90 + 9

23. Show two ways to add these numbers.

a. 23 and 43

b. 45 and 32

24. Solve the given numbers using place value.

a. 98 - 34

b. 56 - 29

c. 98 - 89

d. 72 - 47

Let's Play a Math Game

Things you will need:

➡ Minimum 20 small objects like counters, lego blocks, etc.

➡ A sheet of paper

➡ Pen or pencil to write.

How to play:

1 Place the objects in a bowl.

2 Close your eyes and pick a handful of objects.

3 Now group the objects into pairs and write them in the paper in the template shown below.

Number of objects I picked	Number of pairs I formed	Is the number odd or even

www.prepaze.com

Numbers and Operations in base 10

Each digit in a number has a specific value, three digits in a three-digit number represent the number of hundreds, tens, and ones and 100 can be thought of as a 100 ones or as 10 tens, or as a bundle called a "hundred".

Let's Practice

Representation of Numbers

1. Circle the place value of the numeral in bold.

a) 3**4**

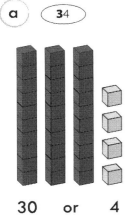

30   or   4

b) 5**2**

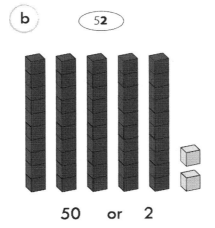

50   or   2

c) **4**5

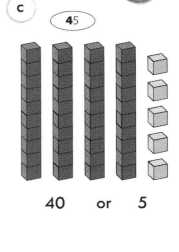

40   or   5

d) 3**8**

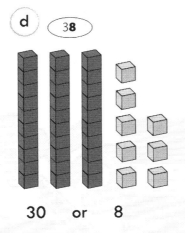

30   or   8

e) **2**1

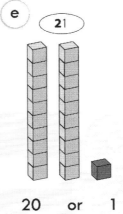

20   or   1

www.prepaze.com

109

prepaze

Hundreds, Tens, and ones

2. Circle the place value of the numeral in bold for the given three-digit numbers.

a) **2**35

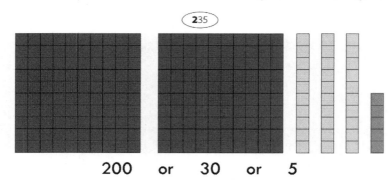

200   or   30   or   5

b) 17**9**

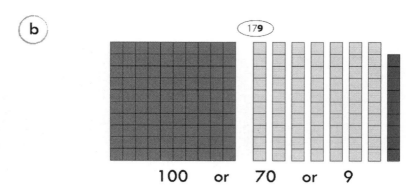

100   or   70   or   9

c) 4**1**2

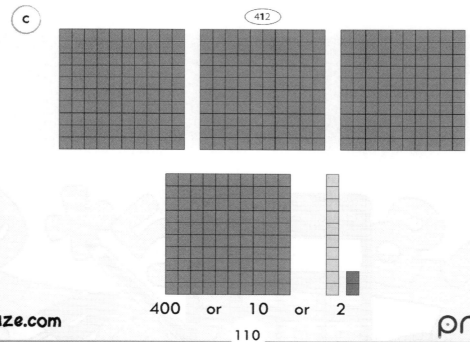

400   or   10   or   2

d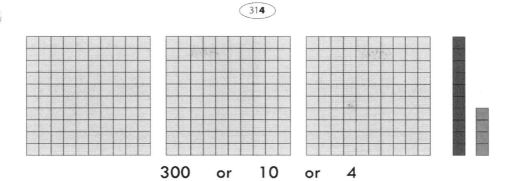

300 or 10 or 4

e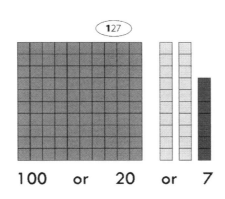

100 or 20 or 7

3. Write the place value of the number.

Number	Hundreds	Tens	Ones
a. 563			
b. 271			
c. 945			
d. 356			
e. 476			

4. Count the hundreds, tens, and ones, and write the correct numerals in the boxes.

a) [   ] Hundreds   [   ] Tens   [   ] Ones

b) [   ] Hundreds   [   ] Tens   [   ] Ones

c) [   ] Hundreds   [   ] Tens   [   ] Ones

d) [   ] Hundreds   [   ] Tens   [   ] Ones

5. Fill in the missing place values.

a. 451 = 400 + 50 + ☐

b. 763 = 700 + 60 + ☐

c. 564 = ☐ + 60 + 4

d. 132 = 100 + ☐ + 2

e. 678 = ☐ + 70 + 8

6. Write the correct number for the number name.

a. One hundred five tens four ones   ☐☐☐

b. Two hundred four tens three ones   ☐☐☐

c. Six hundreds six tens two ones   ☐☐☐

d. Seven hundreds four tens six ones   ☐☐☐

e. Eight hundreds three ones   ☐☐☐

7. Regroup and write the numbers between 0 to 9 in each blank below.

a. 5 tens + 12 ones = _____ tens + _____ ones

b. 7 tens + 17 ones = _____ tens + _____ ones

c. 2 tens + 51 ones = _____ tens + _____ ones

d. 3 tens + 45 ones = _____ tens + _____ ones

e. 3 tens + 63 ones = _____ tens + _____ ones

8. Skip count by 5.

a. 120, 125, 130, 135, _____ , _____

b. 235, 240, 245, 250, _____ , _____

c. 615, 620, 625, 630, _____ , _____

d. 540 , 545, 550, 555, _____ , _____

e. 780 , 785, 790, 795, _____ , _____

9. Skip count by 10 and complete the table.

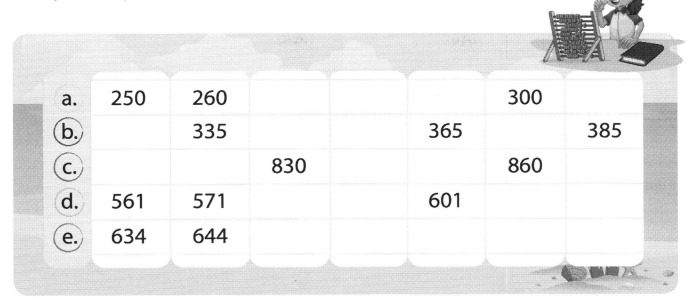

a.	250	260			300	
b.		335		365		385
c.			830		860	
d.	561	571		601		
e.	634	644				

10. Skip count by 100s and fill in the missing numbers.

11. Color the correct number for the number name.

One hundred forty-five

a) 123   145   154

One hundred fourteen

b) 104   114   140

Four hundred fifteen

c) 415   514   541

Five hundred fifty-two

d) 525   550   552

Six hundred seventy-nine

e) 967   769   679

12. Color the correct number name for the number.

112

a) one hundred twelve | one hundred twenty two | one hundred twenty

405

b) four hundred five | four hundred fifty | four hundred fifteen

516

c) five hundred sixteen | five hundred sixty one | five hundred six

645

d) six hundred fifty four | six hundred fifty five | six hundred forty five

809

e) eight hundred ninety | eight hundred nine | eight hundred nineteen

13. Make number bonds to show the hundreds, tens, and ones in each number. Then write the number in unit form. One is done for you.

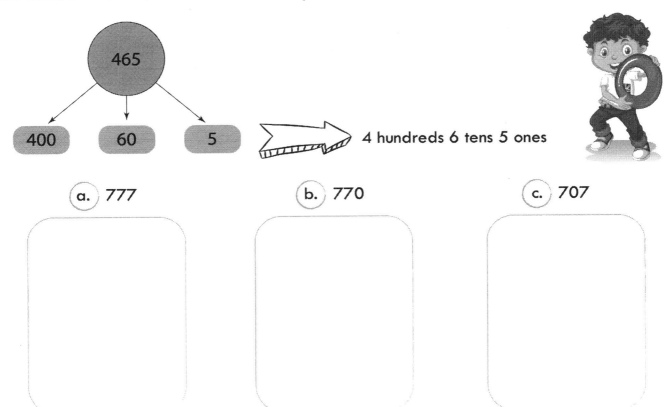

14. Match the number names with the numbers.

430	○	○	One hundred fifty-five
261	○	○	Four hundred thirty
155	○	○	Two hundred sixty-one
617	○	○	Nine hundred
900	○	○	Six hundred seventeen

15. Write in standard form or expanded form as stated.

a. What is 300 + 40 + 5 in standard form? _____

b. What is 200 + 60 + 1 in standard form? _____

c. What is 500 + 70 + 8 in standard form? _____

d. What is 900 + 40 + 3 in standard form? _____

e. What is 800 + 30 + 1 in standard form? _____

f. What is the expanded form of 456 ? _____ +50 + 6

g. What is the expanded form of 109 ? 100 + _____ +9

h. What is the expanded form of 578 ? _____ +70 + 8

i. What is the expanded form of 333 ? 300 + _____ + 3

j. What is the expanded form of 789 ? 700 + _____ + 9

16. Match the given standard form with expanded form.

764	○	○	200 + 6
206	○	○	500 + 50 + 1
551	○	○	700 + 60 + 4
987	○	○	700 + 90 + 9
799	○	○	900 + 80 + 7

Comparison of Numbers

17. Color the correct word to make each sentence true. Fill in the box with >, < or, =. One is done for you.

124 — **is greater than** / is less than / is equal to — 122

124 > 122

a.
153 — is greater than / is less than / is equal to — 135

153 ☐ 135

b.
819 — is greater than / is less than / is equal to — 918

819 ☐ 918

c.
662 — is greater than / is less than / is equal to — 662

662 ☐ 662

d.
735 — is greater than / is less than / is equal to — 753

735 ☐ 753

 **Who is the Greatest?**

18. Write the numbers in order from least to greatest.

a) 312   321   123
___ < ___ < ___

b) 220   202   221
___ < ___ < ___

c) 675   765   567
___ < ___ < ___

d) 823   854   832
___ < ___ < ___

19. Write the numbers in order from greatest to least.

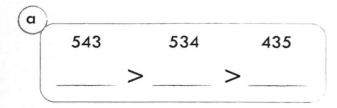

a) 543   534   435
___ > ___ > ___

b) 617   761   661
___ > ___ > ___

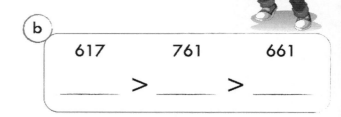

c) 989   899   998
___ > ___ > ___

d) 567   765   734
___ > ___ > ___

Pens and Ice Creams

20. Read the word problems carefully. Write the correct answers in the space provided.

a. The table below shows the number of pens sold at the stationary shop in the last three months.

Number of pens sold	
Month	Number of pens
December	321
January	450
February	445

In which month did the stationary shop sell the most number of pens?

b. The table below shows the number of ice cream cones sold at the ice cream shop each month.

Number of ice cream cones sold	
Month	Number of cones
May	564
June	545
July	559

In which month did the ice cream shop sell the least number of ice cream cones?

21. Solve mentally.

a. 8 ones + _____ = 1 ten   8 + _____ = 10

   8 tens + _____ = 1 hundred   80 + _____ = 100

b. _____ + 3 ones = 1 ten   _____ + 3 = 10

   _____ + 3 tens = 1 hundred   _____ + 30 = 100

c. 1 one + 9 ones = _____ ten   1 + 9 = _____

   1 ten + 9 tens = _____ tens   10 + 90 = _____

   11 tens + 9 tens = _____ tens   110 + 90 = _____

d. 5 ones + _____ = 1 ten   5 + _____ = 10

   5 tens + _____ = 1 hundred   50 + _____ = 100

e. 4 ones + 6 ones = _____ ten   4 + 6 = _____

   4 tens + 6 tens = _____ hundred   40 + 60 = _____

   14 tens + 6 tens = _____ hundreds   140 + 60 = _____

22. Fill in the blanks.

a. 5 ones + 9 ones = _____ tens _____ ones   5 + 9 = _____

   5 tens + 9 tens = _____ hundreds _____ tens   50 + 90 = _____

b. 6 ones + 8 ones = _____ tens _____ ones   6 + 8 = _____

   6 tens + 8 tens = _____ hundreds _____ tens   60 + 80 = _____

c. 7 ones + 9 ones = _____ tens _____ ones   7 + 9 = _____

   7 tens + 9 tens = _____ hundreds _____ tens   70 + 90 = _____

d. 17 ones + 5 ones = _____ tens _____ ones   17 + 5 = _____

   17 tens + 5 tens = _____ hundreds _____ tens   170 + 50 = _____

e. 16 ones + 7 ones = _____ tens _____ ones   16 + 7 = _____

   16 tens + 7 tens = _____ hundreds _____ tens   160 + 70 = _____

Addition and Subtraction

23. Complete the addition sentence. One is done for you.

a. 25 → 30 → 100
    +   +
    5   70

25 + 75 = 100

b. 125 → ____ → ____
    +   +
    5   70

125 + ____ = 200

c. 6 → ____ → ____
   +   +
   4   90

6 + ____ = ____

d. 18 → ____ → ____ → ____
    +   +   +
    2   80 100

18 + ____ = ____

e. 80 → ____
    +
   20

80 + ____ = ____

f. 76 → ____ → ____ → ____
    +   +   +
    4   20 100

76 + ____ = ____

Break Apart

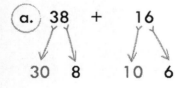

24. Break apart the addends to find the sum. One is done for you.

a. 38 + 16
   /\   /\
 30 8 10 6

Add the tens = 30 + 10 = 40

Add the ones = 8 + 6 = 14

How many in all? 40 + 14 = 54

b. 49 + 5 = ____

Add the ones =

Add the tens =

How many in all?

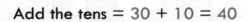

c. 49 + 9 = _____   d. 55 + 45 = _____

Add the ones =   Add the ones =

Add the tens =   Add the tens =

How many in all ?   How many in all ?

e. 67 + 14 = _____   f. 82 + 15 = _____

Add the ones = _____   Add the ones = _____

Add the tens = _____   Add the tens = _____

How many in all ? _____   How many in all ? _____

25. Solve vertically. Draw counters on the place value chart and bundle, when needed. One is done for you.

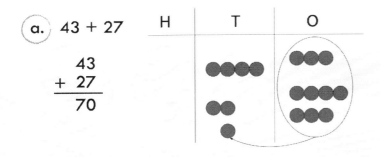

b. 65 + 17

c. 72 + 49

d. 187 + 13

e. 155 + 16

26. Solve the following problems using place value strategies.

a.
$$4 + 7 + 6 = 17$$
$$4 + 7 + 6$$
$$10 + 7 = 17$$

b.
$$3 + 9 + 7 = \underline{\qquad}$$

c.
$$23 + 27 + 15 = \underline{\qquad}$$

d.
$$43 + 55 + 45 = \underline{\qquad}$$

e.
$$37 + 12 + 23 + 28 = \underline{\qquad}$$

f.
$$77 + 35 + 13 + 65 = \underline{\qquad}$$

27. Solve the word problems.

a. Fifty five trees were planted in a garden. Twenty seven more bushes were planted than trees in the garden.

    i. How many bushes were planted?

    ii. How many trees and bushes were planted?

b. The red team scored 15 points less than the green team. Red team scored 35 points.

   i. How many points did the green team score?

   ii. How many points did the red and the green team score altogether?

c. In a small library, there are 456 fiction books and 478 non-fiction books. How many books are there in all?

d. Olivia bought a hand bag for $34, a pair of shoes for $26, a dress for $28, and beauty products worth $22. How much did she spend in all? Show your work.

e. A shopkeeper sold 35 pens on Monday, 53 pens on Tuesday, 47 pens on Wednesday, and 65 pens on Thursday. How many did he sell on all those four days?

28. Solve mentally:

a. 21 + 10 = _____

b. _____ - 10 = 135

c. 91 + 100 = _____

d. _____ -100 = 75

e. 56 - 30 = _____

f. _____ = 140 - 100

g. _____ = 81 - 40

h. 125 + _____ = 145

Solve Using Blocks

29. Subtract using the blocks.

a. 58 - 25

b. 69 - 46

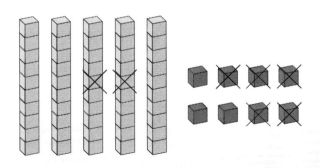

c. 178 - 67

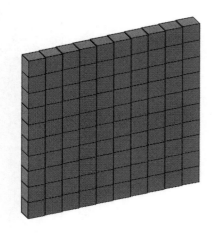

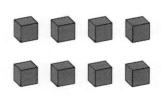

d. 347 - 26

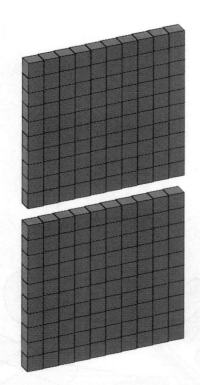
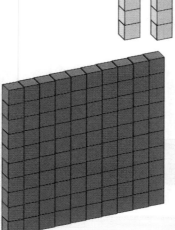
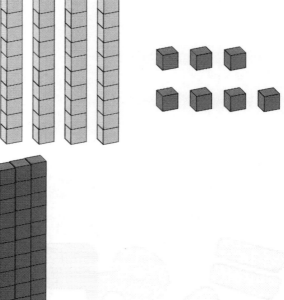

e. 465 - 123

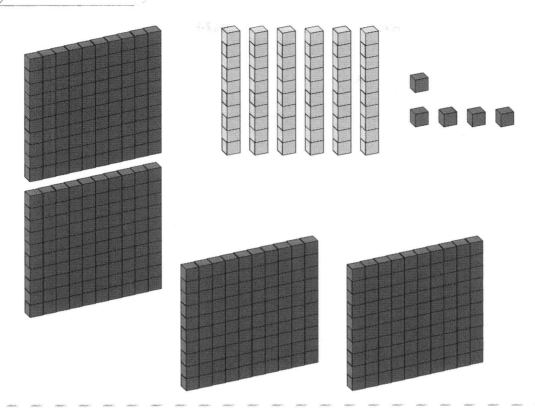

30. Fill in the missing number.

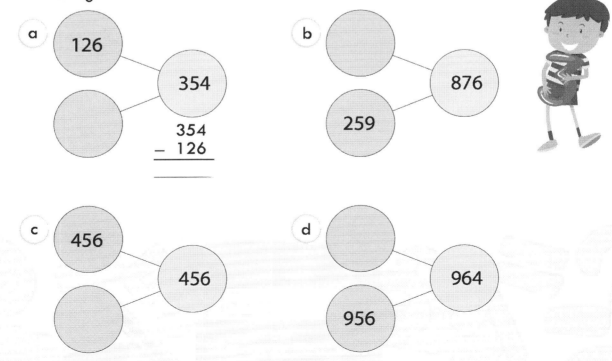

```
  354
-  126
_____
```

31. Solve and show your work with a model. One is done for you.

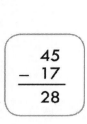
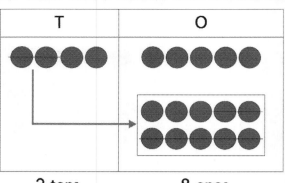

(a) 54 - 18 = _____

(b) 56 - 37 = _____

(c) 65 - 18 = _____

(d) 87 - 18 = _____

(e) 91 - 45 = _____

(f) 77 - 68 = _____

Is William Correct?

32. Look at William's work. Is the subtraction solution correct? Explain your thinking.

William's work:

```
    1 7
  6 7̸
-   4 9
    2 8
```

Explanation:

_____

_____

True or False

33. State whether the number sentence is true or false.

a. Solve 45 - 16 and 67 - 38 vertically.

$$\begin{array}{r} 45 \\ -\ 16 \end{array} \qquad \begin{array}{r} 67 \\ -\ 38 \end{array}$$

45 - 16 = 67 - 38 (**True / False**)

b. Solve 98 - 76 and 90 - 58 vertically.

$$\begin{array}{r} 98 \\ -\ 76 \end{array} \qquad \begin{array}{r} 90 \\ -\ 58 \end{array}$$

98 - 76 = 90 - 58 (**True / False**)

c. Solve 85 - 27 and 67 - 9 vertically.

$$\begin{array}{r} 85 \\ -\ 27 \end{array} \qquad \begin{array}{r} 67 \\ -\ 9 \end{array}$$

85 - 27 = 67 - 9 (**True / False**)

34. Solve the word problems.

a. Jenny collected 87 stamps. She gave away 29 stamps to her brother. How many stamps did she keep with her?

b. Thompson saved $67 and Jack saved $85. Who saved more and by how much?

c. Jackson collected 259 old coins from different countries. John has 128 fewer coins than Jackson. How many coins does Jackson have?

35. Find the solution and model how you found your answer.

   a. 97 + 46

   b. 37 + 58 + 61 + 12 =

36. Write the correct answer in the space provided.

   a.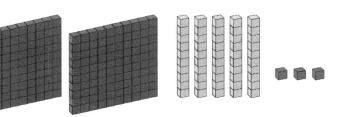

   Which digit is in the ones place in the number above? _____

   b.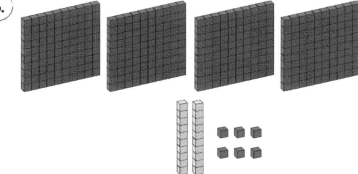

   Which digit is in the hundreds place in the number above? _____

   c.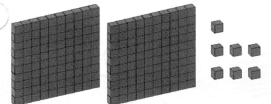

   Which digit is in the tens place in the number above? _____

   d.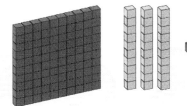

   Which digit is in the tens place in the number above? _____

37. Write the correct answer in the space provided.

a. 1 hundred = _____ tens

b. _____ tens = 2 hundred

c. _____ ones = 4 tens

d. 5 tens = _____ ones

Number Coloring

38. Follow the directions for each problem.

● Shade the number with 1 hundred 0 tens 0 ones

● Shade the number with 3 tens and 2 ones

● Shade the number with 5 tens and 4 ones

● Shade the number with 8 tens and 3 ones

1	2	3	4	5	6	7	8	9	10
11	12	13	14	15	16	17	18	19	20
21	22	23	24	25	26	27	28	29	30
31	32	33	34	35	36	37	38	39	40
41	42	43	44	45	46	47	48	49	50
51	52	53	54	55	56	57	58	59	60
61	62	63	64	65	66	67	68	69	70
71	72	73	74	75	76	77	78	79	80
81	82	83	84	85	86	87	88	89	90
91	92	93	94	95	96	97	98	99	100

39. Choose the correct answer and draw lines to match.

a. A number between 150 and 165.   328

b. A number between 300 and 350.   184

c. A number between 250 and 300.   162

d. A number between 180 and 200.   273

40. Solve the word problems.

a. Steve thinks of a number that has 35 ones and 7 tens. What is Steve's number?

b. Lucy had 8 rolls of pennies, there are 10 pennies in each roll. How many pennies does Lucy have?

c. Jack wants to show the number 20, but he has only 1 ten. How can Jack show the number 20 with only 1 ten?

41. For each box, find and circle two numbers that add up to 120.

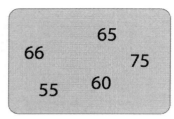
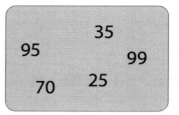

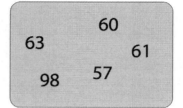

42. The table below shows the top five football teams and their points scored in the last season.

Teams	Points
Wales United	41
Curvy Lions	38
Smart Horses	62
Kind Tigers	49
White Mariners	66

a. How many points did the Smart Horses and the Kind Tigers score together?

b. How many points did the Wales United and the Curvy Lions score together?

c. How many points did the Wales United, White Mariners and the Kind Tigers score together?

_____

d. Which two teams score a total of 90 points?

_____

e. Which two teams score a total of 100 points?

_____

43. Second grade and third grade voted on their favorite ice-cream. The table below shows the number of votes for each ice-cream.

Types of ice-cream	Number of Votes
Caramel ice-cream	46
Strawberry ice-cream	23
Blueberry ice-cream	18
Light Vanilla cream	39
Choco cornetto	44

a. How many more students voted for caramel ice-cream than blueberry ice-cream? Show your work.

b. How many more students voted for light vanilla cream than strawberry ice-cream? Show your work.

c. How many fewer students voted for choco cornetto than caramel ice-cream?

44. Solve the word problems.

a. Rosy has 45 fewer beads than Emma. Emma has 145 beads. How many beads does Rosy have?

b.) Richard collected 189 stickers. His cousin gave him 55 more. How many stickers does he have now?

c.) Camila has $550. After shopping she has $190. How much did she spend?

d.) There were 270 houses in a community. Now there are 540 houses. How many new houses were built?

45. Cecilia and Jammy solved the following problems in different ways. Solve each problem and explain why both ways are correct. One is done for you.

a. 156 - 27

Cecilia:

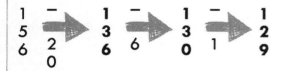

Jammy:

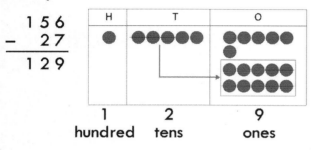

1 hundred   2 tens   9 ones

b. 476 - 47

c. 773 + 287

d. 325 - 143

Measurement and Data

The length of an object can be measured using different tools based on the size of the measured object. Few tools that are used are rulers, yardsticks, meter sticks, and measuring tapes. For example, we use a ruler to measure a book, not a meter tape.

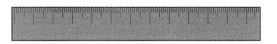

Example

Rina measured the length of a desk in both feet and inches. She found that the desk was 4 feet long. She also found out that it was 48 inches long.

Observe, it only took 4 feet because the feet are so big. It took 48 inches because an inch is a whole lot smaller than a foot.

1 foot											
1 in	1 in	1 in	1 in	1 in	1 in	1 in	1 in	1 in	1 in	1 in	1 in

Time

Different parts of the day are represented using time units like hours and minutes. Clocks have hands that show the hour and minute of the day. There are two types of clock, digital clock and analog clock.

Analog clock   Digital clock

There are 24 hours in a day and each hour has 60 minutes.

Coins and bills have different values. Coins represent a portion of a dollar. $ and ¢ are symbols used to represent an amount of money.

The penny is worth one cent. One hundred pennies make a dollar. One cent can be written 1¢ or $0.01.

The nickel is worth five cents. Twenty nickels make a dollar. One nickel can be written 5¢ or $0.05.

The dime is worth ten cents. Ten dimes make a dollar. One dime can be written 10¢ or $0.10.

The quarter (also called a quarter dollar) is worth twenty five cents. Four quarters make a dollar. One quarter can be written 25¢ or $0.25.

Data

A collection of information in numbers is called data. The collected data can be represented as bar graphs or picture graphs which helps us to interpret and analyze it.

Let's Practice

Measuring and Estimating Length

1. Measure the below objects to the nearest centimeter using the ruler given.

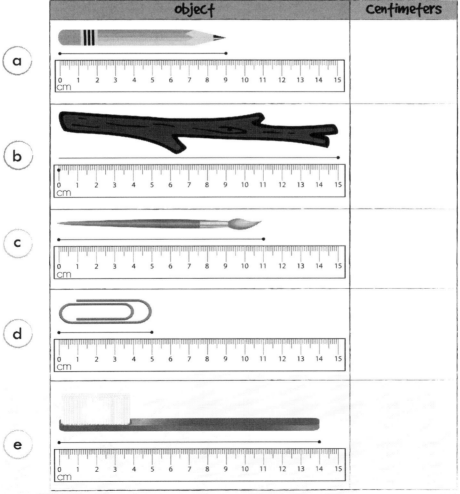

www.prepaze.com
145
prepaze

f. Which is the longest object?

g. Which is the shortest object?

h. By how many centimeters is the shortest object smaller than the longest one?

2. Measure the length of each bar to the nearest inches using a ruler.

about _____ inches

about _____ inches

about _____ inches

about _____ inches

about _____ inches

Ruler or Yardstick

3. Circle the appropriate tool used to measure the following objects.

a. The length of an eraser   12 inches ruler   Yardstick

b. The length of a table   12 inches ruler   Yardstick

c. The length of a room   12 inches ruler   Yardstick

d. The length of a paperclip   12 inches ruler   Yardstick

4. Circle the appropriate metric unit of length for each object.

a. Length of a tennis racket   1 meter   1 centimeter

b. Height of a milk carton   20 centimeters   5 meters

c. Length of an electrical cable   2 centimeters   2 meters

d. Length of a pencil box   1 meter   15 centimeters

5. Measure the length of the cube in centimeters and inches using a ruler.

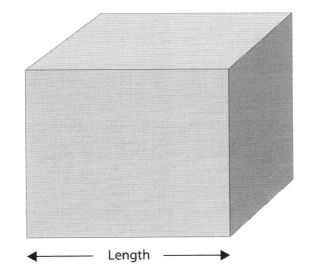

Length

a. The cube is _____ cm long.

b. The cube is _____ inches long.

c. Which is greater? The measurement in number of inches or the measurement in number of centimeters? _____

d. Explain your thinking. _____

6. Read each riddle and tick the appropriate answer.

a. I'm a football. How long do you think I am?
- 11 centimeters
- 11 meters
- 11 inches

b. I am a tennis court. How would you measure my length?
- Measuring tape
- Ruler
- Yardstick

c. I am a caterpillar. How long do you think I am?
- 5 inches
- 2 feet
- 3 meters

d. I am a Christmas tree. How will you measure my height?
- Ruler
- Measuring tape
- Yardstick

e. I am a candle. How tall do you think I am?
- 10 centimeters
- 2 feet
- 1 yard

7. Measure the length of the marked sides of the table in centimeters.

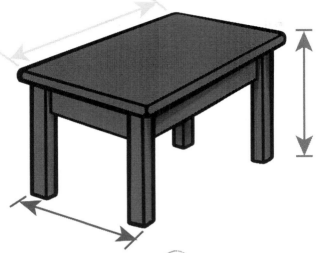

a. Length of the table is _____ cm long

b. Width of the table is _____ cm long

c. Height of the table is _____ cm long

d. Which is longer? And by how much?
_____

8. Estimate the measure of the given objects and fill in the correct unit.
Hint: 1 foot = 12 inch.

a) 4 _____

b) 2 _____

c) 7 _____

9. Measure the height of the shapes below to their nearest inches using a ruler.

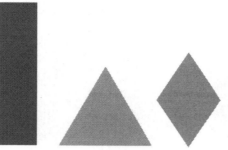

a. Height of the rectangle = _____ inches

b. Height of triangle = _____ inches

c. Height of diamond = _____ inches

d. Which shape is the tallest?

_____

e. Arrange the shapes from the tallest to the shortest.

_____

f. What is the difference between the shortest and the longest shape? _____ inches

g. What is the sum of the heights of all the shapes?

_____

10. Circle the appropriate estimate for each object.

5 meters

15 inches

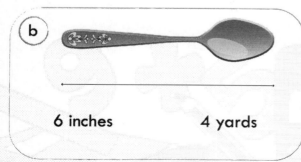

6 inches   4 yards

93 meters

95 centimeters

7 feet

6 yards

www.prepaze.com

150

prepaze

11. If one block represents 2 meters, how long is the below bar?

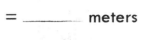 1 block = 2 meters

 = _____ meters

12. Stella has 4 different ribbons.

Ribbon	Length (in meters)
Red	15
Blue	22
Yellow	9
Orange	12

a. What is the length of all the ribbons combined?

_____

b. What is the length of the blue and yellow ribbon together?

c. Would it take more meters or more centimeters to measure the length of each ribbon? Explain your answer.

_____

_____

13. Estimate and then measure the length of the bar using a paperclip and a ruler.

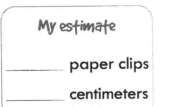

My estimate
_____ paper clips
_____ centimeters

Actual Measurement
_____ paper clips
_____ centimeters

Why are the measurements using paper clips and ruler different? Explain your thinking.

_____

Home Fun

14. Measure the length of any 3 things that you can find in your home in both inches and centimeters. Tabulate your findings.

Object	In inches	In centimeters

Did it take more inches or centimeters to measure the objects? Why?

_____

_____

15. We use meters to measure the longer length and centimeters to measure the shorter length. Will you measure the following objects in meters or centimeters?

a. The distance between the two buildings? _____

b. The length of a mobile phone? _____

c. The length of a crayon box? _____

d. The height of a building? _____

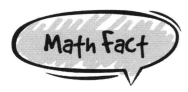

Always remember to leave no gaps, allow no overlays, and start at 0 on a measurement tool while measuring the object.

16. If each square is 1 cm, measure the length of the arrows below:

Length = _____ centimeters

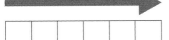

Length = _____ centimeters

Length = _____ centimeters

17. Choose inches, feet, meters or centimeters to fill in the blanks.

a. The length of a school bus is about 40 _____

b. The height of a balloon is about 10 _____

c. The height of the Empire State building is about 380 _____

d. The height of a juice box is about 9 _____

e. The length of a paint brush is about 12 _____

f. The height of a birthday candle is about 2 _____

18. Order the bars from the shortest to the longest.

a)

b)

19. Which is greater?

a. 2 inches or 2 centimeters?

b. 5 inches or 5 yards?

c. 10 centimeters of 10 feet?

d. 16 feet or 16 yards?

e. 12 meters or 12 centimeters?

20. Solve the word problems:

a. 4 students brought strings of ribbons to decorate their class. The lengths of the strings are:

| 15 inches | 23 inches | 8 inches | 19 inches |

What is the total length when the four ribbons are laid end to end?

b. Steve is 48 inches tall. His dad is 70 inches tall. By how much is Steve's dad taller than him?

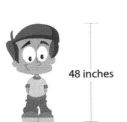

21. Solve the following.

a. Nancy is making a square poster. If each of the sides measure 8 inches, how much washi tape will she need to decorate the sides?

b. The waiting room in the hospital is 56 feet long and 38 feet wide. How much greater is the length than the width?

22. Ann wanted to see how far she can jump on a trampoline. On her first try, she jumped 28 centimeters. On her second try, she jumped 42 centimeters.

a. How many total centimeters did she jump?

b. How many more centimeters did she jump on her second try compared to her first try?

c. On the following day, Ann jumped twice again and made a total of 63 centimeters. What was the difference between her jumps on both the days?

23. Solve the following with the help of the number line given:

a. 10 cars were parked in a parking lot. 7 more cars were parked later in the day. How many cars are there in the parking lot now?

b. Jacky had 23 marbles with her. Her aunt gifted her 13 more marbles. How many marbles did she have in total?

c. There were 62 children in the fair. 18 more children came to the fair. How many are there in the fair now?

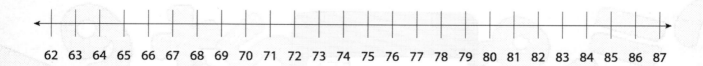

Math With Paper Planes

24. Joey and Jasper were testing their paper airplanes. They fly their planes twice. They record how high their airplanes can fly as shown below:

	Trial 1	Trial 2
Joey's airplane	28 centimeters	33 centimeters
Jasper's airplane	43 centimeters	41 centimeters

a. How far did Joey's airplane fly during trial 1 and trial 2 together?

b. How far did Jasper's airplane fly during trial 1 and trial 2 together?

c. During trial 1, whose plane went far and by how much?

d. During trial 2, what is the difference between the heights reached by both the planes?

25. Adrian was taking a walk in the park. He walked 16 meters and came to the big oak tree. He walked 13 more meters and reached the children's play area. He walked 5 more meters and reached the ice cream stand. How many meters did he walk in all? Use a number line to solve the problem.

Monday or Tuesday?

26. Solve the following:

a. **Monday:** The temperature during the day was 64 degrees celsius. By night time, it was 32 degrees celsius. By how much the temperature dropped by in the night?

_____

b. **Tuesday:** The temperature during the morning was 73 degrees celsius. By how much is the daytime temperature on Tuesday more than that of Monday?

_____

27. Use the number line to find the missing numbers in each number statement below:

a.

5 cm + _____ = 15 cm

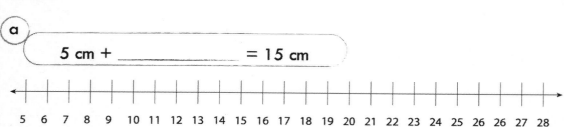

b.

16 inches + _____ = 24 inches

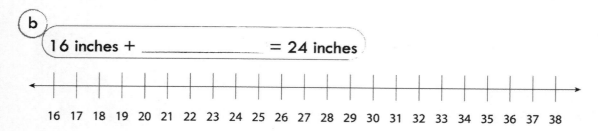

c.

12 feet + _____ = 24 feet

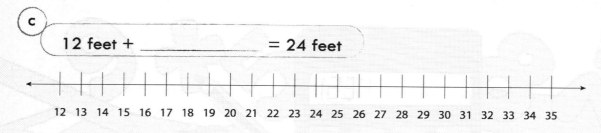

28. Emma wanted to play with her friends. She first went to her friend Josie's house which was 78 meters from her house. Then Emma and Josie went to Stella's house for a birthday party. Stella's house was 43 meters from Josie's house. And if Stella's house is in between Emma and Josie's house, how far is Emma from her home?

29. Solve the following using number lines

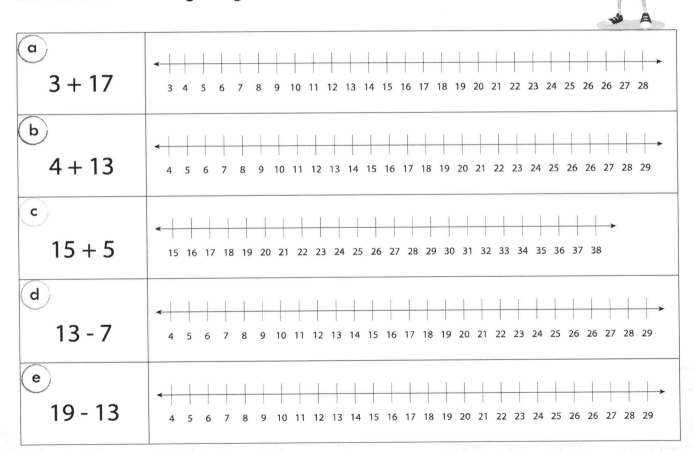

30. Fill in the missing numbers in the number lines below:

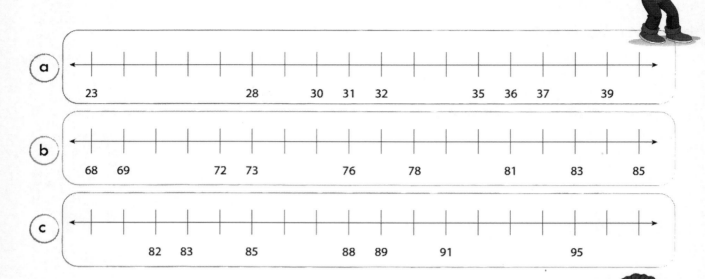

31. Write the number sentence that goes along with the number line plot given:

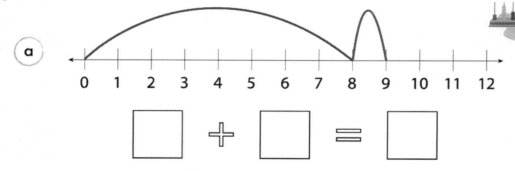

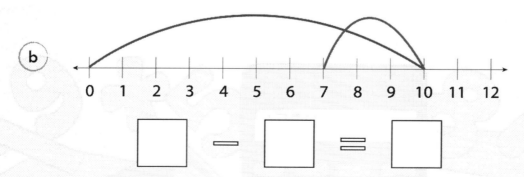

32. Complete the number lines as directed:

a. Counting by 1s

0   1   2   3

b. Counting by 2s

0   2   4   6

c. Counting by 5s

0   5   10   15

d. Counting by 10s

0   10   20   30

33. In each of the following, start from the given number and add 2 to it. Record the sum on the next space in the number line. Continue making jumps of 2 and record the sum in the subsequent places. Continue until all the spaces have been filled.

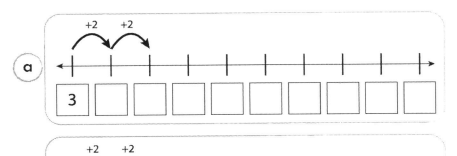

a   3

b   78

34. The distance between Sam's house and the school is 98 meters. The distance between Pricilla's house and the school is 63 meters.

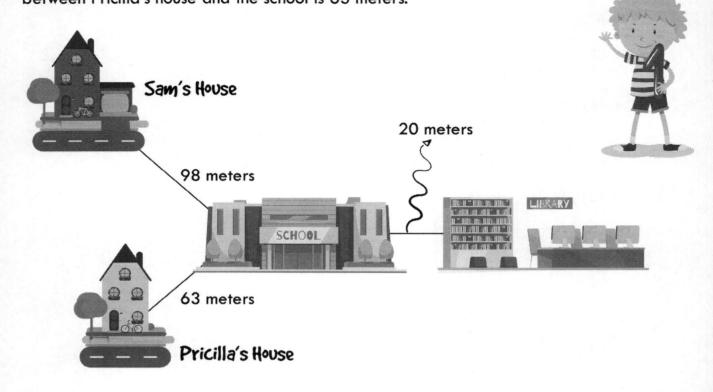

a. If they both start at the same time, who will reach the school first?

_____

b. What is the difference between the two distances?

_____

c. If the library is 20 meters from the school, what is the distance of the library from her home?

_____

35. Mary had 10 stickers with her. Her mom gave her two more stickers. Later that evening, her dad gave her 5 more stickers. Which number line shows how many stickers she had at the end of the day?

a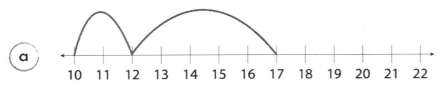

b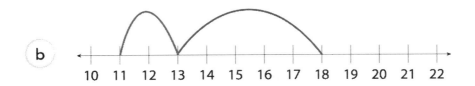

36. Solve the word problems.

a. George has a fishing net that is 50 cm long. He has a fishing rod that is 23 cm shorter than the fishing net. How long is the fishing rod?

b. If Stella cuts her skipping rope into two pieces of length 12 cm and 17 cm, find the length of the original skipping rope.

c. A toy car measures 5 inches. The toy bus is 2 inches longer than the car. What is the length of the toy bus?

37. Solve the word problems.

a.) Lucy made a banana bread that was 40 centimeters. She cut off 21 centimeters to give to her friend. What is the length of the bread she is left with?

b.) The length of a magazine is 15 centimeters. The length of a notebook is 5 centimeters more than the magazine. What is the length of the notebook?

c.) Rick has 36 inches of wooden block and John has 11 inches of wooden block. What is the length of their blocks together?

38. Jance drew a line 10 centimeters long. Hanu drew a line 6 inches long. Jance says her line is longer than Hanu's because 10 is greater than 6. Explain why Jance might be wrong.

_____

_____

_____

39. Read the story problem and answer the question.

Ron and Jessy were cycling in their neighborhood. They started at the same point. In the morning Ron cycled two blocks. In the afternoon, he cycled 3 more blocks and in the evening, he cycled 2 more blocks. Jessy cycled 4 blocks in the morning and 3 blocks in the evening. Now Ron and Jessy were at the same place.

Show how both Ron and Jessy cycled through their neighborhood. Use a number line, starting at 0. Use different colors for morning, afternoon and evening. Write number sentences to support your answers.

Let's Play a Math Game

Things you will need:

➤ Any two measuring tools - Ruler, yard stick, meter stick, measuring tape.

➤ A sheet of paper

➤ Pen or pencil to write.

How to play:

1 Draw an outline of your foot and hand on a sheet of paper.

2 Measure the length using any of the tools.

3 Write them down and compare how the numbers are different when you use different tools.

Time

40. Draw the hands to show the time.

3 o'clock

7 o'clock

8 o'clock

10 o'clock

Analogue and Digital Clocks

41. Match the digital clock and the analog clock that show the same time.

42. Read the clock and write the time to the nearest 5 minutes.

1. _____ 2. _____ 3. _____

43. In a class, students were asked to mark time. Color the correct answer in grey.

5:35   6:05   11:30

44. Match the following.

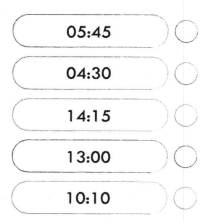   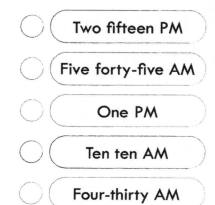

05:45	○	○	Two fifteen PM
04:30	○	○	Five forty-five AM
14:15	○	○	One PM
13:00	○	○	Ten ten AM
10:10	○	○	Four-thirty AM

45. Write the correct time.

Thirty minutes after four	
Ten minutes to two	
Quarter past eight	
Half-past six	

AM or PM

46. Fill in the blanks with 'AM' or 'PM'.

a. I went to see the stars at eight _____ .

b. I had breakfast at seven _____ .

c. I played with my friends at three _____ .

d. I wished my parents goodnight at nine _____ .

Money

Penny, Quarter, Nickel, or Dime

47. Color the correct name for each coin.

a. penny b. quarter c. nickel d. dime	
a. penny b. quarter c. nickel d. dime	
a. penny b. quarter c. nickel d. dime	
a. penny b. quarter c. nickel d. dime	

www.prepaze.com

48. Write the equivalent for each.

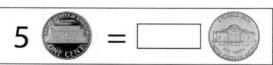
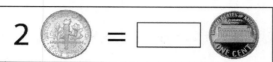
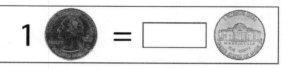
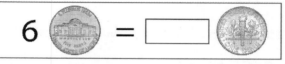

25 [penny] = [ ] [quarter]

49. Write the total amount of money for each.

50. Amy went to the beach. She wanted to buy a ball, a bucket, a shovel, a toy boat, an umbrella and a pair of slippers. Help Amy pay the right amount by coloring the coins needed for each item.

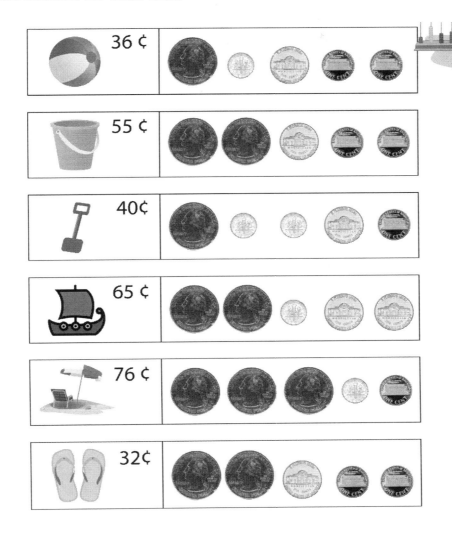

51. Jeff has two quarters, two nickels and a cent. Matt has four nickels, two dimes and ten cents. Who has more money and by how much?

52. Kim has gone to the supermarket. She wants to buy a cupcake costing $2.50 and a sandwich costing $1.50. How much does she need to pay in total?

53. Matt has $5.50 He spends $4. How much money does he have left?

54. Sam took $5 to the movie theatre. Her movie ticket cost $2.25. She bought popcorn for $1.25. How much money does she have left?

55. Complete the sentences.

a) _____ cents make a dime

b) _____ nickels make a quarter

c) _____ dimes make a dollar

Data

56. Count and categorize each picture to complete the table with numbers.

57. Use grid paper to create a picture graph below using data provided in the table. Then, answer the questions.

Varieties of Apple in Jonathan's Fruit shop

Gala	Fuji	Granny smith
🍎	🍎	🍎
12	6	8

Title: _____

Legend _____

a. How many more Gala apples are there than Fuji apples?

_____

b. How many apples are there in all?

_____

c. How many more Granny smith apples are there than Fuji apples?

_____

58. Use the data of Ms. Smith's class vote to create a picture graph in the space provided.

Favorite Pet

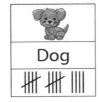 Dog	 Cat	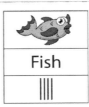 Fish
𝍧 𝍧 |||	𝍧 𝍧	||||

Title: _____

Legend _____

a. How many more students voted for dog than fish? _____

b. How many fewer votes are for fish than cats? _____

c. Write and answer your own comparison question based on the data.

Question: _____

Answer: _____

www.prepaze.com

Sam's Snack Corner

59. Complete the bar graph below using the data provided in the table.

Food items sold at Sam's Snack corner

Cupcake	Hotdogs	Pizza	Burger
7	12	8	6

Title: _____

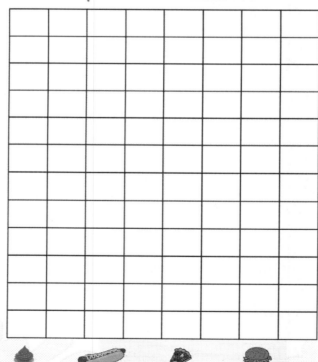

60. Complete the bar graph below using the data provided in the table.

Number of Books Read		
Shirley	Noah	Linda

a. Draw a tape diagram to show how many more books Linda read than Shirley.

b. If Shirley, Noah, and Linda read 32 books altogether, how many books did Noah read?

Title: _____

61. Complete the bar graph using the table with the birds Benjamin spotted at the Corner park. Then, answer the following questions.

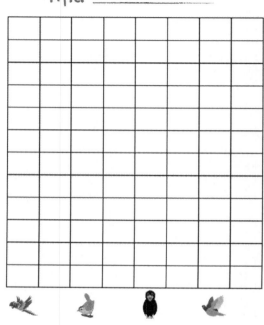

Birds			
Parrot	Sparrow	Crow	Pigeon
7	16	14	9

Title: _____

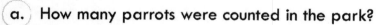

a. How many parrots were counted in the park?

b. How many more crows than pigeons were counted in the park?

c. Which bird was counted half the number of crows?

d. How many birds did Benjamin count in the park?

e. If 5 more sparrows were counted, how many birds would have been counted?

62. The table shows the data of pennies saved by Olivia. Using the data, complete the bar graph. Then, answer the following questions.

Pennies Saved

Monday	Tuesday	Wednesday	Thursday
15	10	4	7

a. How many pennies did Olivia save in all?

b. Her brother saved 18 fewer pennies. How many pennies did her brother save?

c. How much more money did Olivia save on Tuesday than on Wednesday?

d. How will the data change if Olivia doubles the amount of money she saved on Monday?

e. Write a comparison question that can be answered using the data on the bar graph.

Title: _____

Mon   Tue   Wed   Thu

What's Your Favourite Musical Instrument?

63. Steven's Music Store tracks data on their sales of musical instruments. Draw a bar graph to represent the data and answer the questions.

Saxophone	Guitar	Piano	Congo	Trumpet
20	30	10	40	20

a. How many musical instruments were sold in all?

b. Which two instruments were sold in the same number?

c. How many more guitars were sold than trumpet?

d. What is the difference between the sales between Piano and Congo?

64. The height of each student is recorded in inches in the below table. Use the data to create a line plot.

43 inches, 41 inches, 42 inches, 41 inches, 42 inches, 44 inches, 45 inches, 43 inches, 43 inches, 41 inches, 42 inches, 41 inches, 42 inches, 44 inches, 45 inches, 43 inches, 42 inches, 41 inches, 42 inches, 44 inches, 45 inches, 42 inches, 41 inches, 42 inches, 44 inches, 45 inches, 44 inches, 41 inches, 42 inches, 42 inches

65. The below line graph is the height chart showing how much Gina's pet dog weighed each week in pounds.

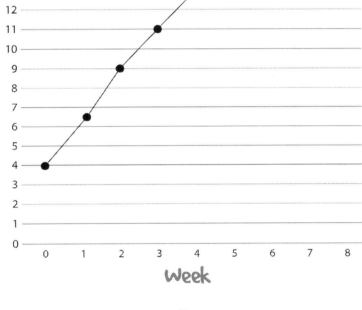

a. How heavy was the dog at 3 weeks?

_____

b. How heavy was the dog at 8 weeks?

c. How much heavier was the dog at 5 weeks compared to 3 weeks?

d. Which week did the dog weigh 18 pounds?

_____

e. How heavy was the dog at birth?

_____

Geometry

Shapes have attributes and properties, which help in understanding the difference between the shapes. Angles, sides, corners are few attributes that define a shape.

Polygon: A closed figure with three or more straight sides. Every side meets exactly two other sides at the corners. A polygon always has the same number of angles as sides.

Triangle: A three-sided polygon with three angles.

Quadrilateral: A four-sided polygon with four angles.

Pentagon: A five-sided polygon with five angles.

Hexagon: A six-sided polygon with six angles.

Triangle   Quadrilateral   Pentagon   Hexagon

There are different types of quadrilaterals.

Quadrilateral: A four-sided polygon with four angles.

Trapezoid: A quadrilateral with at least one pair of parallel sides.

Parallelogram: A quadrilateral with two pairs of parallel sides.

Rectangle: A quadrilateral with four square corners.

Square: A special rectangle with sides that are all the same length.

Rhombus: A quadrilateral with four sides that are all the same length.

Parallelogram   Rectangle   Rhombus   Square   Trapezoid

Smaller shapes can be combined to form bigger shapes and bigger shapes can be decomposed into smaller shapes.

Also new shapes can be formed by repositioning the smaller pieces of the shape.

Let's Practice

1. Match the name of each shape with the words in the word bank.

> Triangle   octagon   Pentagon
>   Square   Hexagon   Rectangle

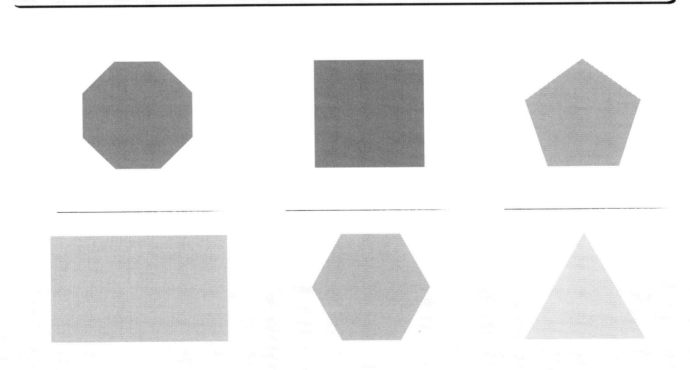

2. Match the 3 - dimensional shape to its name.

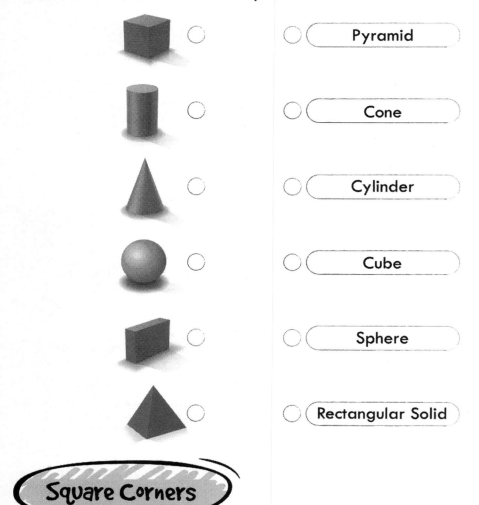

3. Write the number of square corners each shape has:

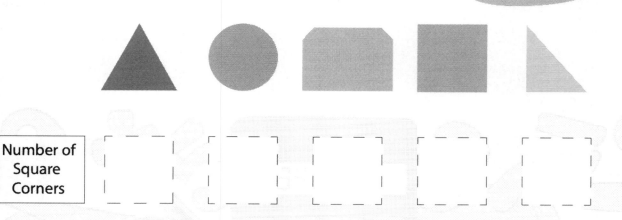

4. What fraction of the shapes are shaded? Write them in the box.

a)

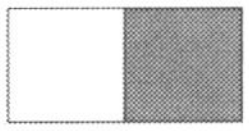

b)

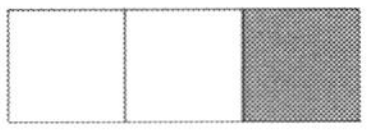

c)

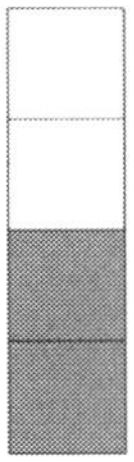

d)

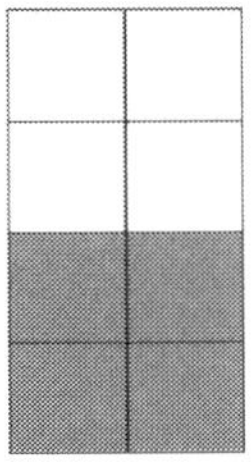

Corners and Sides

5. For each of the shapes below, write how many corners and sides it has:

a)

Number of Sides =_____

Number of Corners =_____

b)

Number of Sides =_____

Number of Corners =_____

c)

Number of Sides =_____

Number of Corners =_____

d)

Number of Sides =_____

Number of Corners =_____

e)

Number of Sides =_____

Number of Corners =_____

f)

Number of Sides =_____

Number of Corners =_____

6. Circle the plane shape that matches the solid shape.

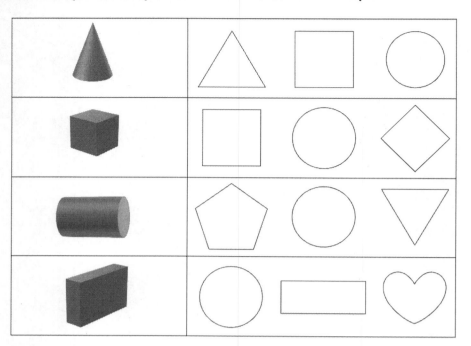

Complete Me!

7. Complete the second half of the objects:

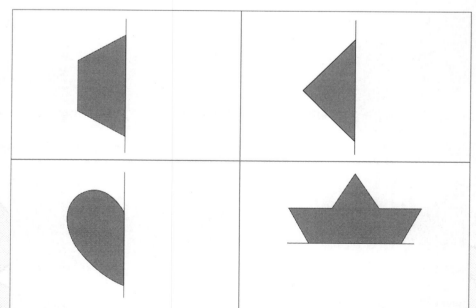

8. Congruent means having the same size and shape. Say if the following sets are congruent or not:

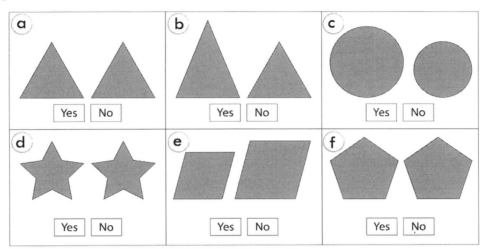

9. Answer the following

a.

There are _____ circles. _____ circles are shaded.

Write the fraction for the shaded part. _____

b.

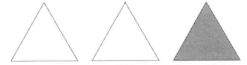

There are _____ triangles. _____ triangles are shaded.

Write the fraction for the shaded part. _____

10. Color the shape for the given fraction.

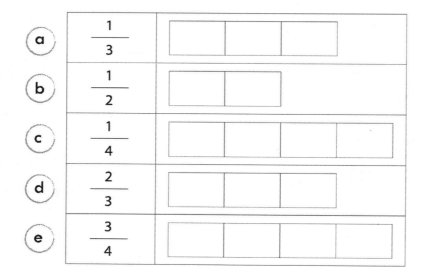

11. Which rectangles have been divided into halves? Circle them.

12. Answer as directed.

   a. Which shape has 4 sides of equal length?   Square or Rectangle

   b. Which shape has fewer corners?   Triangle or Square

   c. Which shape has more sides?   Pentagon or octagon

   d. Which shape has no corners?   Rectangle or circle

13. Look at the given figure and record the number of shapes:

   a. How many rectangles are there? _____

   b. How many triangles are there? _____

14. Follow the steps.

a. Divide the rectangle into 3 rows and 2 columns. How many equal shares can you make?

b. Divide the rectangle into 2 rows and 5 columns. How many equal shares can you make?

15. Match the following.

 a ○   ○ one - eighth

 b ○   ○ one - fourth

 c ○   ○ one - half

 d ○   ○ one - sixth

 e ○   ○ three - fourth

f ○   ○ three - fifth

g ○   ○ one - third

16. Show 2 different ways by which you can divide the rectangles into equal shares.

a. 2 Halves

b. 3 thirds

c. 4 fourths

17. Complete the drawings below to show one whole rectangle.

a. One-half of a rectangle is given. Make it whole by completing the picture.

b. One - third of a rectangle is given. Make it whole by completing the picture.

c. One - fourth of a rectangle is given. Make it whole by completing the picture.

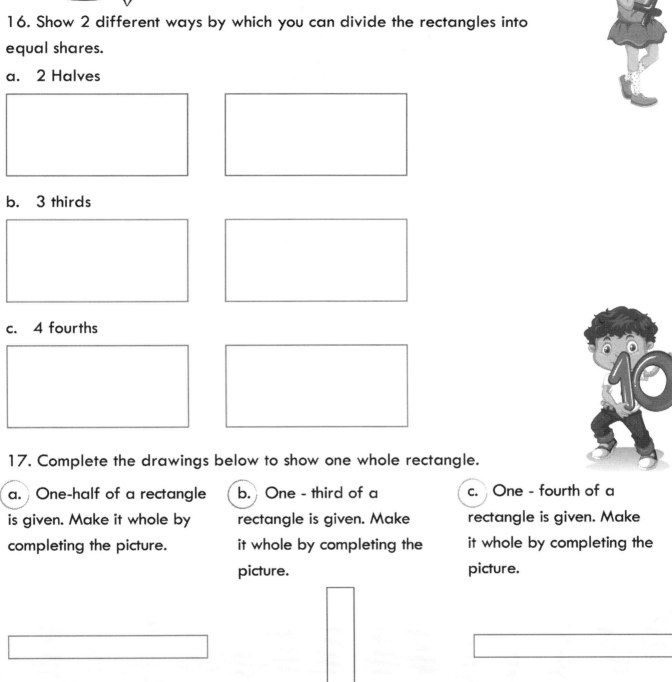

18. Mary, Bret, Jack, and John are sharing a pizza. Divide the pizza so that everyone gets an equal share.

a. What fraction of the pizza did each kid get?

_____

b. What fraction of the pizza did the boys get?

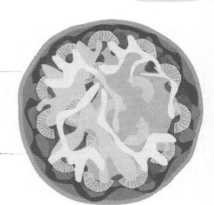

_____

c. If Stella joins in, what fraction will each of the five kids get?

_____

19. Look at the shapes below:

a. What fraction have the following shapes been split into?

_____

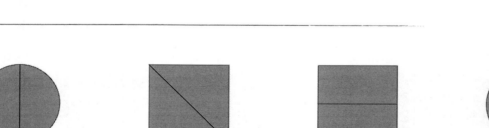

b. Draw 1 more line to divide each shape into one-fourths.

www.prepaze.com

20. Look at the figure below and answer the following:

a. How many squares are there in the figure?

_____

b. How many rectangles are there in the figure?

_____

c. How many triangles are there in the figure?

_____

Science

Help your children learn and enjoy a wide range of information and fun facts that will surprise and amaze them. Find numerous Science experiments, cool facts, activities, and quizzes for the children to enjoy learning.

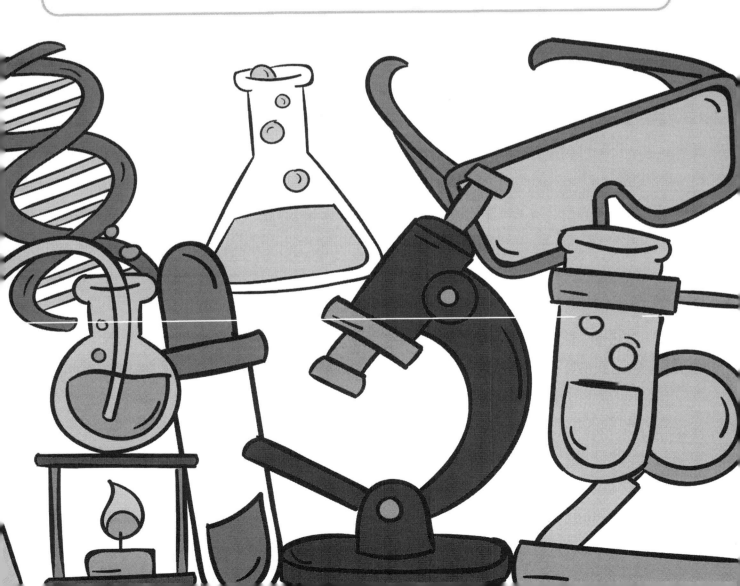

Physical Sciences

Position: the place of an object

Motion: movement or change in position of an object

Speed: distance moved by an object in specific time

Push: to move something away

Pull: to move something closer

Write a sentence to describe the position of the children with respect to the objects in the picture.

 1

 2

3

Types of Force

Identify the type of force in each of these scenarios.

Pedal

- [ ] Push
- [ ] Pull

Open

- [ ] Push
- [ ] Pull

Hang

- [ ] Push
- [ ] Pull

Plank

- [ ] Push
- [ ] Pull

Drag

- [ ] Push
- [ ] Pull

Shop

- [ ] Push
- [ ] Pull

Force

Force has effects on the objects it is applied on in the following ways.

1 Force can make things **move** or **stop** moving things.

2 Force can change the **shape** of an object.

3 Force can change the **direction** of a moving object.

Effects of Force

Identify the effects of force in each of these scenarios.

Push a swing
- [ ] Move or stop
- [ ] Change shape
- [ ] Change direction

Hit the ball
- [ ] Move or stop
- [ ] Change shape
- [ ] Change direction

Dribble the ball
- [ ] Move or stop
- [ ] Change shape
- [ ] Change direction

Pottery
- [ ] Move or stop
- [ ] Change shape
- [ ] Change direction

Model a clay
- [ ] Move or stop
- [ ] Change shape
- [ ] Change direction

Kick a ball
- [ ] Move or stop
- [ ] Change shape
- [ ] Change direction

Magnets

Magnets can pull or attract objects made of **iron**. They can pull through liquids and gases. They can also pull through certain solids like paper and glass. They come in various sizes and shapes.

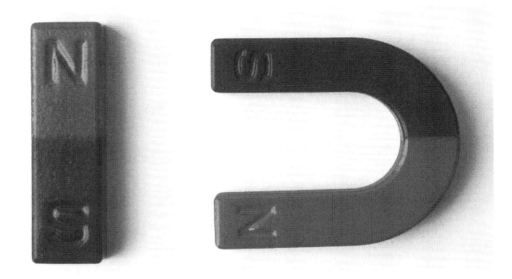

Magnetic force

Magnets have 2 poles - north pole and south pole. A **pole** is a place on a magnet where the magnetic force is the strongest. When two poles are brought together, they either attract or repel each other based on the type of poles in action.

➢ Like poles repel.

➢ Unlike poles attract.

Scavenger Hunt for Magnets

Let's go on a scavenger hunt! Walk around your house with a magnet. Try to attach it to various objects. An object is said to be **magnetic** if it attracts the magnet. Complete the given table.

Name of the object	What is it made up of? (Material of the object)	Is the object magnetic? Yes/No

2. Now that you know the various magnetic objects around the house, take the help of an adult and list 5 devices or appliances in which magnets are used.

I. _____

II. _____

III. _____

IV. _____

V. _____

Attraction or Repulsion?

Tell whether each set of magnets will attract or repel.

☐ Attract
☐ Repel

☐ Attract
☐ Repel

☐ Attract
☐ Repel

☐ Attract
☐ Repel

☐ Attract
☐ Repel

☐ Attract
☐ Repel

☐ Attract
☐ Repel

☐ Attract
☐ Repel

Simple Machines

A **simple machine** is a tool that helps make a force (push or pull) stronger. There are different types of simple machines present in the tools we use in our everyday life.

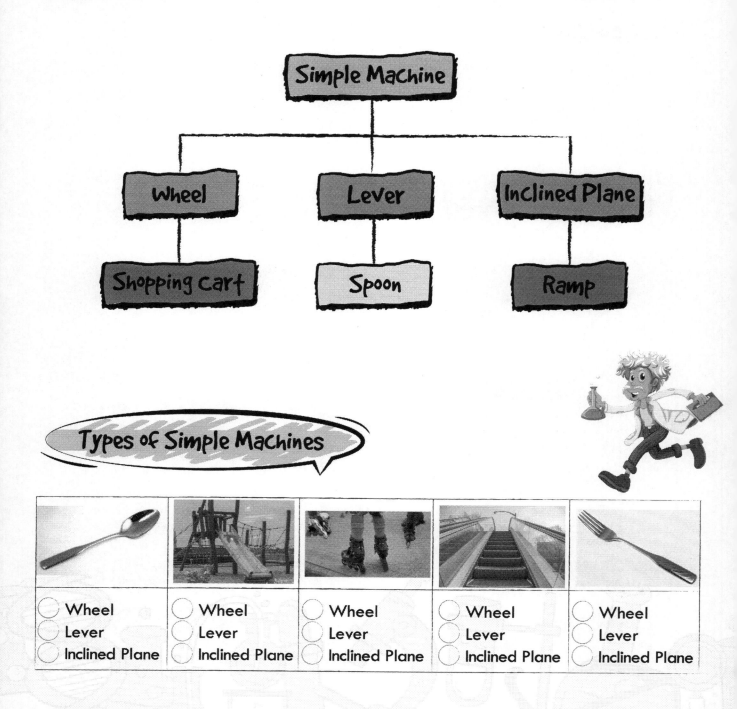

Types of Simple Machines

○ Wheel ○ Lever ○ Inclined Plane	○ Wheel ○ Lever ○ Inclined Plane	○ Wheel ○ Lever ○ Inclined Plane	○ Wheel ○ Lever ○ Inclined Plane	○ Wheel ○ Lever ○ Inclined Plane

Simple Machines Around Us

1. Circle and name the different simple machines you can identify in this picture.

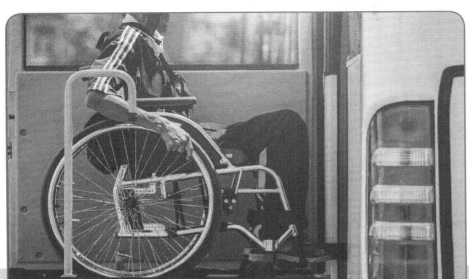

2. Write one other tool/application for the given simple machines.

   a. Wheel - _____

   b. Inclined plane - _____

   c. Lever - _____

The force that pulls things towards each other is **Gravity**. The gravitational force of an object is directly proportional to its size. That means, larger the object, stronger is its force of gravity.

Since Earth is larger than other things on its surface, its gravity is the strongest here.

True or False?

State whether the following statements about gravity are true or false.

1. The Earth's gravity does not have any effect on humans.	
2. The strength of gravity of an object depends on its size.	
3. There is no gravity on high mountain peaks.	
4. Gravitational force cannot be seen.	
5. When a ball is thrown, it falls back to the ground because of the ball's gravity.	

Draw arrows to show the direction in which Earth's gravitational force is acting on objects.

Did You Know?

A scientist by the name **Sir Isaac Newton** was the first to discover gravity.

The story tells how Newton was under an apple tree in his garden, and an apple fell on his head. This got him thinking about what makes objects fall to the ground and not float upwards.

He later realised that every object attracts every other object.

Newton named this force as gravity. This is a derivation from a Latin word 'gravitas' which means **weight**.

Sound Energy

Sound: the kind of energy we can hear

Vibrate: to and fro movement

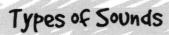

Types of Sounds

Snap fingers — ☐ Loud ☐ Soft

Playing drums — ☐ Loud ☐ Soft

A barking dog — ☐ Loud ☐ Soft

A duck's quack — ☐ Loud ☐ Soft

Knocking the door — ☐ Loud ☐ Soft

People on a roller coaster — ☐ Loud ☐ Soft

Sounds Around Us

Walk around your neighbourhood. Identify and categorise the different sounds you hear.

Loud Sounds	Soft Sounds

➥ Friction is a force that slows down moving things.

➥ It always occurs between two things rubbing on each other.

➥ There is more friction on a rough surface than on a smooth surface.

➥ Friction can be useful, like when we are cycling.

➥ We also try to reduce friction as it does not help in a certain scenario, like when we are on a water slide.

Gravity vs Friction

Circle the pictures that show gravity and tick the pictures that show friction.

Uses of Friction

Identify if friction is useful or not useful in each of these scenarios.

- [ ] Useful
- [ ] Not useful

- [ ] Useful
- [ ] Not useful

- [ ] Useful
- [ ] Not useful

- [ ] Useful
- [ ] Not useful

- [ ] Useful
- [ ] Not useful

- [ ] Useful
- [ ] Not useful

www.prepaze.com

Energy Word Grid

Find answers for the following clues in the word grid.

1. The energy we hear
2. The place of an object
3. Move an object away from you
4. Distance moved by an object in a specific time
5. How far away is one object from another?
6. Move an object closer to you
7. Change in position
8. A force that slows down moving objects
9. Not loud
10. A simple machine that helps you roll objects instead of lifting them
11. A spoon is an example of this simple machine
12. When a hitter hits an incoming ball, it changes the _____ of the ball.

W	H	E	E	L	O	D	P	W	S
S	E	F	F	J	A	I	O	I	O
P	J	R	W	Q	V	S	S	S	U
E	D	I	R	E	C	T	I	O	N
E	E	C	P	U	S	A	T	F	D
D	P	T	U	V	V	N	I	T	I
X	U	I	L	M	C	C	O	B	E
V	S	O	L	H	W	E	N	A	V
E	H	N	T	V	N	Y	U	K	E
M	O	T	I	O	N	Y	Q	X	R

Life Sciences

Name the Young Ones

What are the young ones of these animals called?

Animals	Young Ones
Dog	
Cat	
Cow	
Hen	
Duck	
Butterfly	
Sheep	
Deer	
Horse	
Goose	

Match the animals with their young ones.

Reproduction in Animals

Identify the type of reproduction in the animals.

☐ lays eggs
☐ gives birth to young ones

☐ lays eggs
☐ gives birth to young ones

☐ lays eggs
☐ gives birth to young ones

☐ lays eggs
☐ gives birth to young ones

List 5 more animals of each type.

Lays Eggs	Gives Birth to Young Ones

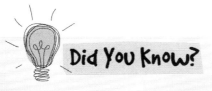

Did You Know?

External, visible part of the ear that you can touch and bend is called **pinna**. All animals, including humans, that give birth to young ones, also known as **mammals**, have this pinna or external ear.

Now go back to the previous and check if this is true.

Reproduction in Plants

Mark the parts of the plant and circle the parts that help in reproduction.

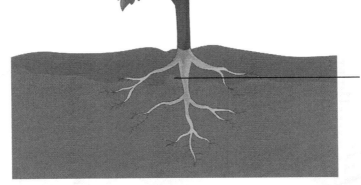

Lifecycle of a Butterfly

Identify and explain the different stages of the lifecycle of a butterfly.

Lifecycle of a Frog

Identify the different stages in the lifecycle of a frog.

Did You Know?

The dramatic change that a frog undergoes from when it breaks out of an egg until it reaches adult stage is called **metamorphosis**. Here, the baby looks entirely different from its adult stage. Another animal that undergoes metamorphosis is the butterfly.

1. Draw a picture of a rainforest and a desert in the given space.

Rainforest

Desert

2. Write 3 words to describe:

Rainforest	Desert
1. _____	1. _____
2. _____	2. _____
3. _____	3. _____

3. Write 3 animals found in:

Rainforest	Desert
1. _____	1. _____
2. _____	2. _____
3. _____	3. _____

Structure of Plants

Differentiate between plants in a rainforest and a desert as shown in the images.

Criteria	Rainforest	Desert
Leaf		
Stem		
Appearance		
Examples	1. 2.	1. 2.

Taking after Parents

Stick a picture of yourself in the space given below and answer the questions that follow.

Paste your photo here

1. How do your features resemble your father's?

2. How do your features resemble your mother's?

3. What other ways do you take after your father?

4. What other ways do you take after your mother?

5. Which parent do you think you resemble the most?
- [ ] Father
- [ ] Mother

Germination

Color the image and name the different parts of a germinating plant.

Lifecycle of a Plant

Identify the different parts involved in the lifecycle of a plant.

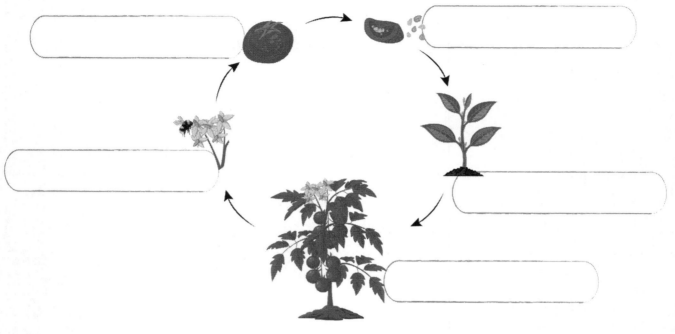

Seed Dispersal

We know that seeds cannot move from one place to another, unlike animals. At the same time, all the seeds cannot grow in the same place and need to be distributed all over. This is carried out by factors like the **wind, water, animals,** and **explosion** of pods. This is called **dispersal of seeds.**

The seeds have specific adaptations for each mode of dispersal. Not all seeds can be dispersed by all methods.

Modes of Seed Dispersal

Observe the different types of seeds and match them with their mode of dispersal.

Seeds	Mode of Dispersal
 ○	○ **ANIMALS**
 ○	○ **EXPLOSION**
 ○	○ **WIND**
 ○	○ **WATER**

www.prepaze.com

Earth Sciences

What are Rocks Made of?

Minerals: what rocks are made of

Property: defines qualities of an object

Weathering: how wind and water change the shape of rocks

Soil: made up of tiny rocks and biotic matter

Fill in the missing letters in the names of minerals.

1. F __ LD __ __ AR
2. M __ C __
3. __ L __ R T __
4. Q __ A __ T
5. G __ __ D
6. __ O __ P __ R
7. T __ L __
8. A __ UMI __ __ M

Identify the Minerals

Draw lines to match the pictures and uses of minerals with their names.

I am found in watches.

Diamond

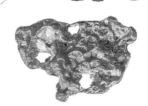

I am used to make pennies.

Lead

I am used to make jewellery.

Quartz

I am a precious mineral. I am used in drilling.

Aluminium

I am found in pencils.

Gold

I am used to make construction materials and machinery.

Copper

Properties of Minerals

Observe the minerals and draw lines to match them with their property.
Note: Each mineral may have one or two of these properties.

 ○   ○ Shiny

 ○

 ○ Dull

 ○

 ○ Hard

 ○

 ○   ○ Soft

Agents of Weathering

Observe the following images of rocks and identify the agents of weathering.

_____

_____

_____

_____

_____

Composition of Soil

Shake up the soil!

Let's do a simple activity to know that soil is made up of different kinds of tiny rocks.

What you need:

- A glass jar with lid
- A spoon
- A fork
- Water
- A whiteboard marker or tape

What to do:

Step 1 Use the fork and spoon to loosen the topsoil.

Step 2 Dig about 4 inches, and collect a cup of soil.

Step 3 Add the collected soil into the jar filling upto one-third.

Step 4 Fill the jar with water upto the neck.

Step 5 Close the jar tightly.

Step 6 Shake the jar for a few minutes.

Step 7 Set the jar down on a table. Leave it undisturbed.

Step 8 In a while you will notice large particles of sand settle down at the bottom of the jar. Mark the top of this layer with the marker or tape. Label it as sand.

Step 9 About an hour later, look for a layer of smaller particles that settle over the layer of sand. Mark the top of this layer with the marker or tape. Label it as silt.

Step 10 Leave the jar undisturbed overnight.

Step 11 You will notice the water is clear and another layer of even smaller particles have settled over the layer of silt.

Step 12 Mark the top of this layer with the marker or tape. Label it as clay.

Step 13 If there are any plant and animal bits, you will find it usually floating over the clear water.

www.prepaze.com

What I see:

Draw and fill this jar picture to show what your jar looks like. Also, label the different layers.

What I know:

Soil is made of _____ (same/different) kinds of tiny rocks and bits of

_____ and _____ .

Kinds of Soil

Identify the different kinds of soil and complete the table.

What does the soil look like?			
Name of the soil			
Colour of the soil	☐ Light brown ☐ Dark brown ☐ Red ☐ Black	☐ Light brown ☐ Dark brown ☐ Red ☐ Black	☐ Light brown ☐ Dark brown ☐ Red ☐ Black
Texture	☐ Clay ☐ Clumpy ☐ Grainy	☐ Clay ☐ Clumpy ☐ Grainy	☐ Clay ☐ Clumpy ☐ Grainy
Water retention	☐ High ☐ Low	☐ High ☐ Low	☐ High ☐ Low
What does it have?	☐ Iron ☐ Tiny bits of plants ☐ Tiny bits of animals ☐ Grainy bits of rocks	☐ Iron ☐ Tiny bits of plants ☐ Tiny bits of animals ☐ Grainy bits of rocks	☐ Iron ☐ Tiny bits of plants ☐ Tiny bits of animals ☐ Grainy bits of rocks
Growth of plants	☐ Not much ☐ Most plants ☐ Few plants	☐ Not much ☐ Most plants ☐ Few plants	☐ Not much ☐ Most plants ☐ Few plants

www.prepaze.com

prepaze

Fossil: remains of plants and animals that lived in the past
Paleontologist: a person who studies fossils
Extinct: living things from the past that do not exist anymore

Answer the following questions in one word.

1. What is a person who studies fossils called?

2. What is an animal said to be when it is no longer found to be living on Earth?

3. What is a full set of bones of an animal called?

4. Give an example of an animal that is extinct.

5. What is the remains of an animal from the past called?

6. Approximately how many years does it take for a fossil to be formed?

7. Give one reason why animals become extinct.

8. What is the place in California called where millions of animal and plant fossils are found?

9. Name one animal from millions of years ago whose fossil was found in California.

10. What is a person who studies rocks called?

www.prepaze.com

DIY Fossil

Make your own fossil.

What you need:

- A cup of all-purpose flour
- Half cup salt
- 2 teaspoons instant coffee
- Water
- Baking paper

What to do:

Step 1 Mix the flour, coffee, and salt in a bowl.

Step 2 Add water in portions and knead a perfect dough. It should be wet, but not sticky. Check for a play dough consistency.

Step 3 Take portions of the dough and make small palm-sized balls.

Step 4 Place a dough ball on the baking paper and flatten it with your palm.

Step 5 Use the dinosaur toys and make imprints on the flattened dough balls by pressing the toy gently.

Step 6 If you have small toys, you could imprint the entire toy into the flattened dough ball.

Step 7 The fossil is now ready.

www.prepaze.com

Step 8 There are two methods to dry your fossil.

> a. **Air dry** - let the fossil out in the open for it to dry and harden. This will take days or weeks to happen, depending on the weather.
>
> b. **Oven dry** - With the help of an adult, bake your fossils in an oven, at the lowest temperature setting, for 3-4 hours. Leave it to cool. Fossils will harden more when cooled.

 Step 9 Use your fossils to decorate your room. Alternatively, you can challenge your friends to match the fossils with the toys.

 Did You Know?

Did you know that poop can be fossilised too?

Fossils of poop are called coprolites, and they can tell us what the animal ate.

The fossils of teeth, along with coprolites can tell us if the animal is a herbivore (plant-eater), carnivore (meat-eater) or an omnivore (eats both plants and animals).

Coprolites of Tyrannosaurus rex has been found to have pieces of bones which says that T-rex ate other animals.

 Natural Resources

Natural resources: things from the earth that people make use of

Examples: water, minerals, wind.

Sources of Food

Where do these foods come from? Draw lines to match the foods with their source.

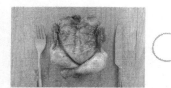

PLANT

ANIMAL

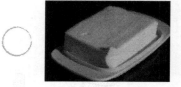

Uses of Natural Resources

How are natural resources used? Draw lines to match the natural resources on the left with the things we get from them.

Tree		Electricity
	Minerals	
Water		Furniture
	Energy	
Mountain		Jewelry
	Wood	
Soil		Food
	Wool	
Wind		Clothes
	Energy	
Animal		Electricity
	Crop	

www.prepaze.com 233 prepaze

Investigation and Experimentation

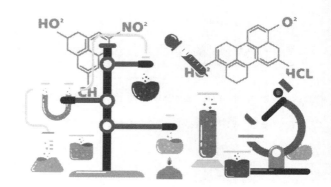

Make a Recipe Card

Let's cook! Find out the recipe for mashed potatoes from adults or the internet and make your own recipe card here.

Try out your recipe with the help of an adult and draw what your dish looks like here.

Routine Journal

Record your daily routine here. List the time and description of at least 10 things you do throughout the day.

Time	Activity

Bar Graph

John, Scott, Susan, Tom, and Serena are in a library reading their favourite books. The number of pages they have completed so far is given in the table below.

Name	Pages
John	24
Scott	40
Susan	64
Tom	32
Serena	48

Draw a bar graph to represent the given data. Name the axes appropriately.

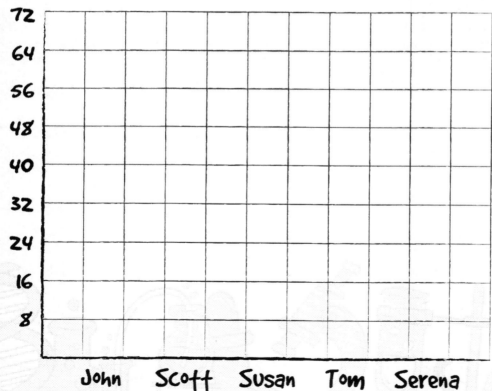

www.prepaze.com

Make predictions for the given conditions for a seed to grow.

Growing Conditions		Prediction
Water	Sunlight	(What do you think will happen?)
✓	✓	☐ The seed will germinate and grow well ☐ The seed will germinate, may or may not grow well ☐ The seed will not germinate
✓	✗	☐ The seed will germinate and grow well ☐ The seed will germinate, may or may not grow well ☐ The seed will not germinate
✗	✓	☐ The seed will germinate and grow well ☐ The seed will germinate, may or may not grow well ☐ The seed will not germinate
✗	✗	☐ The seed will germinate and grow well ☐ The seed will germinate, may or may not grow well ☐ The seed will not germinate

Answers

English Answer Key

Collective Nouns

Unscramble the Words

Rearrange the scrambled letters to make collective nouns.

1. POD
2. SWARM
3. PACK
4. HERD
5. FLIGHT
6. SCHOOL
7. BROOD
8. GAGGLE
9. LITTER
10. BLOCK

Choose the Best Answer

1. The school hired a **band** of musicians for the party.
2. We saw a **flock** of sheep in the fields.
3. She climbed a long **flight** of stairs.
4. A **pod** of dolphins swam past the ship.
5. The players of our **team** played well.

Pair It Up

Match the collective nouns to the respective nouns.

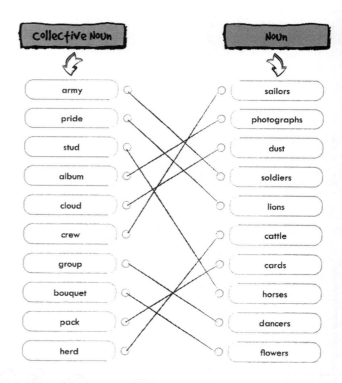

Irregular Plural Nouns

Underline the Plural Nouns

1. Pete cleaned his desk and put the **books** on the **shelves**.

2. The **trees** shed **leaves** during fall.

3. Ron has lost four **pens** so far.

4. I always brush my **teeth** before going to bed.

5. The **monkeys** were swinging on the branch.

Make Plural Nouns

Use the plural form of the words in the parentheses.

1. dice
2. women
3. oxen
4. potatoes
5. puppies
6. glasses
7. pouches
8. fish
9. toys
10. geese

Irregular Verbs

Match the present tense and past tense verbs.

Present Tense	Past Tense
make	found
cry	ran
tell	swam
take	taught
swim	made
teach	took
find	cried
run	told

Conjugate

Complete the sentence with the irregular forms of the verbs given in the parentheses.

1. ate
2. saw
3. sang
4. shut
5. bought
6. rose
7. heard
8. set
9. spread
10. knew

Coloring Fun

Color the picture. Then add an adjective for each word taken from the picture. Answers may vary

The given table lists adjectives. Fill in the most appropriate adjective for each word in the balloon.

Read the sentences and circle the adjectives

1. **big**- describes the noun elephants

2. **bitter**- describes the noun coffee

3. **prickly**- describes the noun quills

4. **oval**- describes the noun park

5. **noisy**- describes the noun classroom

6. **sharp**- describes the noun knife

7. **blue**- describes the noun eyes

8. **mild**- describes the noun earthquake

9. **thoughtful** - describes the noun gift

10. **happy** - describes the noun Andrea

1. Sheila brought a **healthy** snack.
Explanation: Healthy is the adjective that describes the noun snack.

2. She bought a **grey** car.
Explanation: Grey is the adjective that describes the noun car.

3. I had to carry the **heavy** box.
Explanation: Heavy is the adjective that describes the noun box.

4. It was a **warm** day in spring.
Explanation: Warm is the adjective that describes the noun day.

5. My father cleaned up the **messy** garage.
Explanation: Messy is the adjective that describes the noun garage.

6. The anaconda is the **largest** snake in the world.
Explanation: Largest is the adjective that describes the noun snake.

7. Alex ate **six** slices of the pizza.
Explanation: Six is the adjective that describes the noun pizza.

8. The **black** cat climbed up the tree.
Explanation: Black is the adjective that describes the noun cat.

9. There are **millions** of stars in the universe.
Explanation: Millions is the adjective that describes the noun stars.

10. The child was playing with a **colorful** ball.
Explanation: Colorful is the adjective that describes the noun ball.

Sensory Words

Describe Me

Each food item shown below has a unique taste. Write the most appropriate adjective that describes it.

juicy   crunchy/salty   crunchy/salty   creamy   bitter

spicy   fizzy   sweet   flaky   buttery

Look at the pictures and write down the best word from the table that describes each of them.

1. I could not hold the ice cube because it was **cold**.
2. The skin of a pineapple is **prickly**.
3. I wore mittens as the pan was **hot**.
4. One side of the sandpaper is **rough**.
5. Ben plays with his **soft** teddy bear.
6. Please draw with a **sharp** pencil.
7. I love that **silky** scarf.
8. My fingers were **sticky** after I dipped them in sugar syrup.
9. The marbles were **smooth**, so they rolled over the table.
10. The cake became **hard** because the oven was too hot.

Read the sentences and fill in the blanks with correct words from the box.

creaky; **deafening**; **silent**; **faint**; **shrill**; **squeaky**

The sense of smell is just as important. Guess the adjective that describes the smell of the picture best.

fresh   stinky   delicious

smoky   rotten   stale

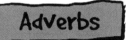

Underline the adverbs in each sentence.

1. The tortoise trundled along **slowly**.
Explanation: slowly- describes the verb **trundled**.

2. The hare ran **faster** than the tortoise.
Explanation: faster- describes the verb **ran**.

3. I went **inside** to get my umbrella.
Explanation: inside- describes the verb **went**.

4. The mailman carried the package **carefully** to the car.
Explanation: carefully- describes the verb **carried**.

5. Nina slept **peacefully**.
Explanation: peacefully - describes the verb **slept**.

6. The dog barked **loudly** at the mailman.
Explanation: loudly- describes the verb **barked**.

7. Mike and Rita have **always** been best friends.
Explanation: always- describes the verb **been**.

8. It snowed **heavily** during Christmas.
Explanation: heavily- describes the verb **snowed**.

9. Ben **quietly** walked behind mother.
Explanation: quietly- describes the verb **walked**.

10 The kitten purred **happily**.
Explanation: happily- describes the verb **purred**.

honestly, soon, playfully, near, and **quietly**
Explanation: The words describing verbs are adverbs.

Rewrite the sentences by changing the wrong adjective or adverb.

1. You must read the instructions **carefully**.
Explanation: Carefully is an adverb that describes the verb reading.

2. When I saw him last, he was sitting **comfortably** in the chair.
Explanation: Comfortably is an adverb that describes the verb sitting.

3. The **loud** noise woke me up.
Explanation: Loud is an adjective that describes the noun noise.

4. Dan **quietly** entered the room.
Explanation: Quietly an adverb that describes the verb entered.

5. That man is wearing **smelly** socks.
Explanation: Smelly is an adjective that describes the noun socks.

6. The **calm** people waited in line.
Explanation: Calm is an adjective that describes the noun people.

7. My uncle bought me a **delicious** candy.
Explanation: Delicious is an adjective that describes the noun candy.

8. Mr. Connors drove us to the park in his **new** car.
Explanation: New is an adjective that describes the noun car.

Add adjectives and adverbs to these sentences to make them more informative and interesting. One is done for you.

Answer may vary

Choose the best answer

1. My friends and I
Explanation: The beginning of a sentence and the pronoun I are capitalized.

2. Mount Everest
Explanation: The name of a place is capitalized.

3. San Jose
Explanation: The name of a place is capitalized.

4. Abraham Lincoln
Explanation: The name of a person is capitalized.

5. me, Tuesday
Explanation: The day of the week is capitalized.

Rewrite the sentences applying capitalization rules.

1. Jane, Tina, and I are going out to play.
Explanation: Jane and **Tina** have to be capitalized as they are names of people. The word **I** has to be capitalized.

2. Dr. Tucker said we could visit him on Monday.
Explanation: Dr. is a title. **Tucker** is the name of a person. **Monday** is a specific day of week.

3. Elaine's family is going to Disneyland for spring break.
Explanation: Elaine is the name of a person. **Disneyland** is the name of a place.

4. She worked at Spencer's Supermarket.
Explanation: She is capitalized as it is the beginning of a sentence. **Spencer's Supermarket** is the name of a place.

5. I saw Ron walk past.
Explanation: I is capitalized as it is a pronoun. **Ron** is the name of a person.

Add commas where necessary.

1. I had soup, a sandwich, and a cake.
Explanation: Comma is added as it is a list.

2. If we leave now, we can reach on time.
Explanation: Comma is added to pause between two ideas.

3. Mark said, "I am glad you could come!"
Explanation: Comma is added to pause before quotes.

4. I told her, but she forgot.
Explanation: Comma is added between two independent clauses.

5. Yes, it is her watch.
Explanation: Comma is added after an introductory word.

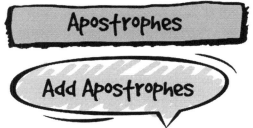

The following sentences lack apostrophes. Add apostrophes wherever necessary.

1. He's been sick for a week now.
Explanation: Apostrophe used as a contraction for **He is**.

2. This is someone else's bag.
Explanation: Apostrophe used to answer the question "Whose?"

3. Why's the dog barking?
Explanation: Apostrophe used as a contraction for **Why is**.

4. I have borrowed Gary's watch.
Explanation: Apostrophe used to answer the question "Whose?"

5. The movie, The Lion King, was released in '94.
Explanation: Apostrophe used to denote the year 1994.

Write down the contractions of the words using apostrophes.

Words	Contractions
I would	I'd
I am	I'm
you are	you're
are not	aren't
It is	it's
Let us	Let's

Read the passage and add commas and apostrophes where necessary.

One foggy morning, Jane and Ken went out for a walk with Ken's dog, Buddy. As they walked slowly, Buddy scampered ahead. Jane spotted a mushroom and said, "This is an ant's umbrella!" Ken looked at the dewdrops on the leaves and said, "This is the ladybug's water cooler!" Right then, Buddy picked up a bone and barked, "Woof! This is a lucky dog's breakfast!"

Spelling Patterns

Read the paragraph given below and write down the words that have **ir**, **er**, **ur**, and **ear**. Say the words aloud and find out how they are similar.

Words with er	Words with ir	Words with ur	Words with ear
Chester	third	curly	year
sister	birthday	purple	
Jennifer	thirteenth	furry	
Jefferson	skirt		
December			
Esther			
together			

Read the paragraph given below and write down the words that have **oy, oi**. Say the words aloud and find out how they are similar.

Words with oy	Words with oi
Joyce	joined
soy	tinfoil
enjoys	spoiled
foyer	boils
boys	points
royal	joints

Here are some words related to Easter. Circle the correct spellings.

happy, candy, bunny, basket, eggs, Sunday

Choose the correct spelling.

1. Be **nice** to each other. (nice/nise)

2. My **house** is close by. (houce/house)

3. The fox jumped **over** the fence. (over/ower)

4. The **box** is full of books. (bocks/box)

5. The **rope** to draw water from the well is very old. (roap/rope)

6. There was a strange **bird** at my window. (bird/burd)

7. Get **off** my bike. (of/off)

8. She is wearing a new **coat**. (coat/cote)

9. It might **snow** today. (snoe/snow)

10. We put up our **tent** at 9 '0 clock. (tant/tent)

Each sentence has an underlined word. Two words are provided on either side of the sentence. Circle one word which has the same meaning as the underlined word.

penned - wrote; wealthy - rich; cruel - mean; sweltering - hot; nibbled on - ate slowly; curious - wanting to know; toppled - fell over; repeat - say again; prepare - make ready; dozes - sleeps

Understand the context and complete the sentences with the most appropriate word from the table.

1. The student gave a **witty** answer to the teacher.

2. They offered **beverages** like milk, tea, and coffee.

3. The dog ran when he was let off the **leash**.

4. When Amy answered back, her mother **glared** at her.

5. The **aroma** of spaghetti made my mouth water.

6. The florist sells **various** flowers in summer.

7. Michael Jordan has an **immense** fan base.

8. The mouse was caught **beneath** a block of wood.

9. The crow was **perched** on the tree.

10. The fireflies **glimmer** in the far away fields.

Find the meaning of the underlined words. Write down what you think the meaning of the word is.

1. shaking

2. drink other than water

3. arithmetic operation to find the difference between numbers

4. having no living members

5. comes near

Root Words

Write down the root word of every word underlined.

friend; hop; fast; shame; sleep; thank; appear; teach; speak

From the root word given, guess the correct word using the context and fill in the correct word.

1. lucky

2. unable

3. enjoyable

4. smartest

5. incorrect

Compound Words

Missing Words!

Form compound words with the help of the pictures given.

pancake
butterfly
newspaper
waterfall
cartwheel
crosswalk
starfish
bathtub
sunflower
lunchbox

Spot the Compound Words

Underline the compound words used in each sentence.

1. The **mailman** was on time.
2. The **rainbow** has seven colors.
3. Rex plays **basketball** every other day.
4. This is Easter **Sunday**.
5. She added mint to **watermelon** juice.
6. The warm **sunshine** woke me up this morning.
7. The first **snowfall** of the year is always beautiful.
8. Aunt Tanya put the wrong key in the **keyhole**.
9. I turned on the **flashlight** when the power went out.
10. Mom bought **everything** that was on the list.

Shades of Meanings

Arrange each set of words in the order of strength. The strongest being on the top of the list.

cheerful, happy, thrilled
glanced, saw, stared
bothered, angry, furious
warm, hot, sizzling
tired, drained, exhausted
nibble, eat, devour
sip, drink, gulp
like, love, adore

Reading: Literature
Unity Is Strength

Complete the words.

1. food
2. banyan
3. hunter
4. help
5. chewed

Match the pigeons' feelings to the action

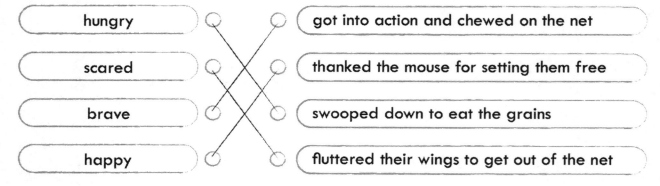

- hungry — swooped down to eat the grains
- scared — fluttered their wings to get out of the net
- brave — got into action and chewed on the net
- happy — thanked the mouse for setting them free

Sequence the sentences in the correct order

4	The pigeons decided to fly away with the net.
6	The mouse chewed the net and set them free.
2	They swooped down to eat the grains.
7	They thanked the mouse and flew away together.
5	They flew to a village to find their friend, a mouse.
1	A flock of hungry pigeons saw some grains scattered under the banyan tree.
3	They were trapped in the net spread by a hunter.

www.prepaze.com

prepaze

What do you think would have happened if....

(Tick the answer you find most appropriate.)

1. a
2. a
3. b

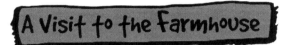

A Visit to the Farmhouse

Story Elements

1. The characters in the passage are: Frankie, Bony, Bobby, Timmy, Joey and Aunt Mona.

2. Joey was the naughtiest among them.

3. The cousins were excited about their visit to Aunt Mona's farmhouse.

4. Aunt Mona had planned an Easter egg hunt for them at the farmhouse.

5. Joey climbed the roof of the stable and fell through the roof onto a stack of hay.

6. The horses helped Joey when he was in trouble.

7. Aunt Mona was glad that Joey did not get hurt.

Guess the Meaning

Choose the closest meaning of the words printed in bold font in the context of the passage.

onset - beginning

excited - thrilled

schedule - plan

outdoor - outside

collapsed - fell

trouble - difficulty

narrated - told

escaped - set free

Mother Earth

Poem Appreciation

1. Garbage

2. Swoon

3. Homebase

4. The "other" living beings are plants and animals-other than human beings.

5. The poet says the Earth will give you more clean air, fresh water, and rich soil.

6. The poet wants the readers to understand how we, as humans, need to keep the Earth clean by disposing of garbage responsibly.

1. the author
Explanation: The author is the part of the narration, hence the pronoun "I" is used.

2. first person
Explanation: The writing is in first person as the narrator is the part of the story.

3. in spring
Explanation: The time of the story is given in the beginning of the passage.

4. They ran back home.
Explanation: When it poured, they ran back indoors (home).

5. They were not able to complete their walk due to rain.
Explanation: The following lines have the clue: Rocco, lay at my feet, whimpering and whining occasionally. I told Rocco that I was just as disappointed as he was. This shows that they were disappointed as they were not able to go for a walk.

6. on the horizon
Explanation: They saw the rainbow on the horizon.

7. elated
Explanation: The narrator was happy in the end, which is evident by the line "Totally worth the wait."

8. unhappy
Explanation: The word disappointment means being unhappy as something did not happen as one had hoped.

9. pleasant
Explanation: whimpering means: making unhappy noises; peeked means: to look in a sneaky way; pleasant means: happy and enjoyable.

10. to entertain us by sharing an experience
Explanation: Narrative writing is such as this one is meant to entertain the readers.

Read the given narrative and identify the introduction, sequence of events and the solution/ending and the conclusion. Write it down in the template provided.

Narrative

Topic: A rainy morning walk

Title: The rainbow

Catchy first sentence:
Spring had just set in. Flowers were blooming and leaves were sprouting on trees

Event 1
Walking the dog while it was drizzling outside. Started raining so had to return home.

Event 2
We waited for an hour and it stopped raining. We went out again.

Event 3
Spotted a beautiful rainbow.

Last sentence:
Beauty of the rainbow made the one-hour wait totally worth it.

Reading: Informational Text

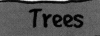

1. The main purpose of the passage is to educate readers.
Explanation: The author is educating readers on conservation of trees.

2. The most frequently used word in this passage is trees.
Explanation: Trees appear in almost every other sentence.

3. both a and b
Explanation: birds, lizards, and squirrels use the tree as home.

4. Trees give as shade and oxygen
Explanation: This statement is true according to the passage. Option (a) is false because there are more uses of trees besides making furniture. Option (c) is false because according to the passage, lizards and squirrels also live in trees.

5. Trees fill the air with carbon dioxide.
Explanation: This statement is false. The trees fill the air with carbon dioxide according to the last paragraph.

In the table, list two key details and reasons that support the author's view in the passage.

Important Point	Key Detail	Reasons/Evidences
Trees are a boon to all living things.	Trees are home to animals.	birds squirrels, lizards
Trees are a valuable part of our surroundings.	Trees give a lot of things.	shade, nuts and fruit wood
Trees should not be cut down.	Trees help keep living things alive.	take in carbon dioxide and give out oxyge

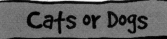

1. to help the readers understand which pet is suitable for them

Explanation: The passage explains the pros and cons of both cats and dogs to help the readers understand which pet would be suitable for their convenience.

2. cats
Explanation: The second paragraph of Cats as Pets directly states that they are easier to take care of.

www.prepaze.com

3. third person
Explanation: The consistent use of the pronoun "they" show that the writing is in third person.

4. hear a mouse in a hole
Explanation: Cats have a sharp hearing capacity. They can hear a mouse in a hole, while humans can't.

5. being given a bath
Explanation: Most dogs hate a bath.

Compare and Contrast

Fill in the important points, key details, and reasons in the table comparing the passages on cats and dogs.

	Title	Important Point	Key Detail	Reasons/Evidences
Passage 1	Cats As Pets	Cats are great pets.	Cats are a joy to be around.	cuddle up and purr
			Cats are easy to take care of.	no need to be bathed. lick themselves clean
			Cats use litter boxes.	
			Cats have sharp hearing capacity.	Can hear a mouse in a hole
			Cats sleep a lot.	About eighteen hours a day.
Passage 2	Dogs As Pets	Dogs are wonderful pets.	Dogs are happy and cheerful animals.	cuddly and like to be petted show feeling with their tails
			Dogs need to be bathed.	hate a bath
			Dogs need to be walked.	
			Dogs have sensitive noses.	Can sniff out a mouse, insect or stranger around the house.
			Dogs are light sleepers.	Alert even while sleeping. Always ready to go!

Go through the table you just filled out and write down the similarities and differences between the information given in the two passages.

Compare and Contrast

Cats As Pets & **Dogs As Pets**

Cats | Dogs

Similarities

Easy to take care of

Use litterbox

Sharp hearing capacity

Sleep a lot

Wonderful pets
Cuddly

Need to be bathed

Need to be walked

Have sensitive noses

Light sleepers

Pizza

Read and Answer

1. pizza
Explanation: The answer can be found in the opening statement.

2. three
Explanation: regular, deep-dish, or thin crust are the 3 types mentioned in the passage.

3. to share his or her opinion on preferred pizza
Explanation: The passage is about the author's preference in pizza.

4. The author prefers it as it has toppings of his/her choice.
Explanation: Out of the three choices, this is the valid reason as the author says this is the reason why he/she prefers deep dish pizza.

5. the audience
Explanation: After giving his/her opinion, the author is speaking directly to the audience in the last sentence, "Don't you agree?"

Fact or Opinion

opinion

Topic: Pizza

Opinion: I love pizza.

Reason 1	Reason 2	Reason 3
Lots of cheese	Get to pick the toppings	Can make it as spicy as I want it to be

Conclusion: Variety in crust, toppings - pizzas makes a great meal.

Read the sentence in each balloon. If it is an opinion, color the balloon grey. If it is a fact, color the balloon black.

For each word frame a sentence which states a fact and one that states an opinion.

Word	Fact	Opinion
chips	Chips are snacks.	Potato chips taste better than corn chips.
roses	Stems of roses have thorns.	Yellow roses are beautiful.
chocolate	This store has a separate aisle for chocolate.	Dark chocolate is the best.
parrot	Some parrots can talk.	Parrots are fun as pets.
music	Music improves memory.	I like instrumental music.

Explanation: Answers may vary.

Life cycle of a Hen

Understanding Text

1. 3 weeks
2. to warm the eggs and keep the temperature in the proper range
3. 3 months
4. after a year
5. five stages
6. both a and b

Study the Illustration

Use the picture on the right and the words given in the box to complete the sentences below.

sunlight; water; carbon; dioxide; sugar; oxygen

Reading: Foundational Skills

Long and Short Vowels

Spot the Vowels

Underline the vowel in the following words

b<u>o</u>x; h<u>a</u>nd; ch<u>ai</u>r; ch<u>e</u>rr<u>y</u>; p<u>ai</u>nt; p<u>e</u>t; s<u>u</u>n; p<u>i</u>cnic; c<u>a</u>ke; y<u>a</u>rn; j<u>u</u>g; p<u>u</u>mpk<u>i</u>n; f<u>i</u>sh; ch<u>i</u>ck<u>e</u>n; k<u>e</u>ttl<u>e</u>; <u>e</u>leph<u>a</u>nt

Explanation: answer may vary

a. bat

b. fell

c. dish

d. fog

e. fuss

Readout each word given below. Pay attention to the sound of the vowels in these words. These are long vowel sounds. Write down one word that contains the long vowel.

Explanation: Answer may vary.

a - carrot

e - see

i - bite

o - sow

u - June

Spelling and Sound

Read out each word given below. Pay attention to the sound of the vowels in these words. These are short vowel sounds. Write down one word that contains a short vowel.

Read out what each picture shows and circle the word.

snow; boat; pin; oval; rose

Use **a, ai,** or **ay** to spell the word given in the picture.

cake, rain, hay

Use **ea, ey,** or **ee** to spell the word given in the picture.

peas, three, honey

Use **i, igh,** or **ie** to spell the word given in the picture.

night, pie, kite

Use **o, oa,** or **ow** to spell the word given in the picture.

goat, pot, tow

Use **u, ue, oo,** or **ou** to spell the word given in the picture.

goose, ruler, glue, house

Now that you have learned the long vowel sounds, identify as many long vowel words in the table of letters given.

BITE, CUBE, GOAL, KEEP, KEY, LAKE, MOON, MOUTH, PAY, POLE, TEACH, THROW, TIGHT

Fill in the blanks.

1. clown
2. soup
3. seat
4. mouse
5. mow
6. beach
7. pouch
8. feet
9. monkey
10. coat

Two-Syllable Words

On either side of the word, write the two syllables that make up the word.

pa - per

cap - tain

sea - son

pea - nut

mo - tel

Complete Me!

Fill in the correct words from the box to complete the sentence.

1. The **sky** is always blue in the month of July.
2. I am going to fly to New York **City**.
3. The baby crawled after the **ball**.
4. The girl was **pretty** and shy.
5. I cannot **write** on the board with a white marker.

Prefixes and Suffixes

Connect the Puzzle Pieces

Draw a line to connect the appropriate prefixes and suffixes to make meaningful words.

friendly; misunderstood; eating; careful; unbutton; dislike; fearless; walked; preheat; strongest

Fill in the blanks with the appropriate prefix from the table.

6. She was **un**able to attend the ceremony.
7. Lyle **dis**owned the book.
8. Dad said, we will **re**paint the house this summer.
9. Grandma wears **bi**focal glasses.
10. Some countries have a **tri**color flag.
11. The shopkeeper has to **re**pay us for the faulty toaster.
12. Please **un**lock the door for me.
13. I bought a **pre**paid calling card.
14. A shape with three sides is a **tri**angle.
15. The stranger was **mis**led by the locals.
16. We have a **bi**monthly payment plan.
17. Help me **un**wrap the gift.
18. **Pre**cook the apples for ten minutes.
19. Do not **dis**obey the traffic rules.
20. You cannot **mis**use this laptop

Math Answer Key

Numbers

Odd and Even Numbers

1. a. Not even, since the objects cannot be divided into equal groups of 2.

   b. Even, since the objects can be divided into equal groups of 2.

   c. Not even, since the objects cannot be divided into equal groups of 2.

   d. Even, since the objects can be divided into equal groups of 2.

2. a. 46 books. Adding 34 comic books and 12 story books totals to 46 books.

   b. 21 tomatoes. Subtracting 24 tomatoes from 45 tomatoes gives 21 tomatoes.

   c. a. 35 oranges. Subtracting 24 from 59, we get 35 oranges.
   b. 94 fruits. Adding 59 apples and 35 oranges we get 94 fruits in total.

3.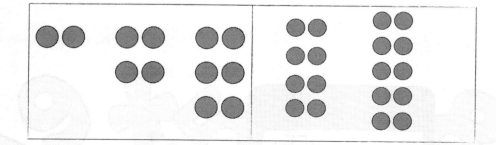

4. There are **9** twos. There are **0** left over.

www.prepaze.com

Arrays

Decorate with Balloons

5.

Possible solution 1

An array with 6 rows and 3 columns.

> There are **6** rows. There are **3** columns.
>
> There are **even** (even/odd) numbers of objects.

Possible solution 2

An array with 3 rows and 6 columns.

> There are 3 rows. There are 6 columns.
>
> There are **even** (even/odd) numbers of objects.

6. Skip counting by 2 we get, 4, 6, 8, 10, 12, 14, 16, 18, 20

7. a. 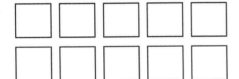 b. 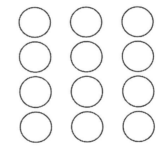 c.

   d.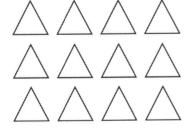

8. a. 3 rows of 4 = 12; 4 + 4 + 4 = 12   b. 5 columns of 4 = 20; 4 + 4 + 4 + 4 + 4 = 20

   c. 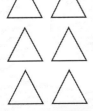 or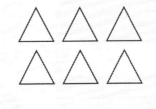

9. 2 rows of 4 = 8
    4 + 4 = 8

    4 columns of 2 = 8
    2 + 2 + 2 + 2 = 8

10. a. 5 rows of 3 = 15
    b. 3 columns of 5 = 15
    c. 5 + 5 + 5 = 15
    d. 10

11.
    a. 2 rows of 3 = 6
    b. 3 columns of 2 = 6
    c. 2 + 2 + 2 = 6

12.
    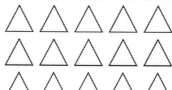

13. The expressions are : 5 + 5 and 2 + 2 + 2 + 2 + 2

14. a.
    12 chairs
    3 + 3 + 3 + 3 = 12

    b.
    6 windows
    3 + 3 = 6

    c.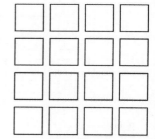
    16 cards
    4 + 4 + 4 + 4 = 16

15.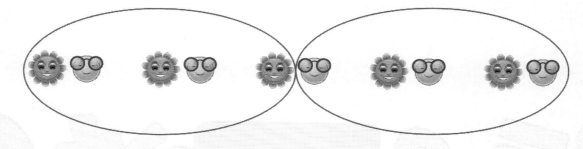

16. Jake used the place value method and Ronnie directly added with carry over. Both types will give us the same answer.

The Flower Pot Problem

17. a. 3 rows of 4 = 12
     b. 4 columns of 3 = 12
     c. 4 + 4 + 4 = 12
     d. 16

Who Won the Game?

18. a. 25 points
     b. 22 points
     c. Ash - 11 points
        Danny - 27 points
        Frank - 19 points

19. A possible solution is

Spot the Odd One

20.

21. a.

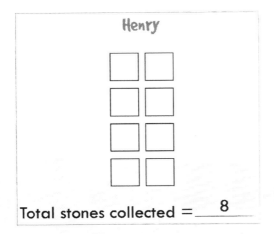

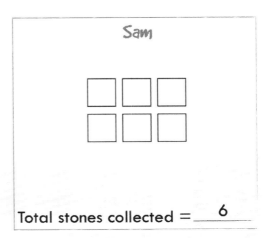

b. Henry

22. Add like units for the given numbers. One is done for you.

a. 76 + 23

```
   76
+  23
-----
   09
   90
-----
   99
```

b. 23 + 32

```
   23
+  32
-----
   05
   50
-----
   55
```

c. 28 + 49

```
   28
+  49
-----
   17
   60
-----
   77
```

d. 90 + 9

```
   90
+  09
-----
   09
   90
-----
   99
```

23. Show two ways to add these numbers.

a. 23 and 43

```
   23
+  43
-----
   06
   60
-----
   66
```

```
   23
+  43
-----
   66
```

b. 45 and 32

```
   45
+  32
-----
   07
   70
-----
   77
```

```
   45
+  32
-----
   77
```

24.

a. 98 - 34
```
  98
- 34
  ──
  04
  60
  ──
  64
```

b. 56 - 29
```
  56
- 29
  ──
  07
  20
  ──
  27
```

c. 98 - 89
```
  98
- 89
  ──
  09
  00
  ──
  09
```

d. 72 - 47
```
  72
- 47
  ──
  05
  20
  ──
  25
```

Representation of Numbers

1. a. 30
   b. 2
   c. 40
   d. 8
   e. 20

Hundreds, Tens, and Ones

2. a. 200
   b. 9
   c. 10
   d. 4
   e. 100

3.

Number	Hundreds	Tens	Ones
a. 563	500	60	3
b. 271	200	70	1
c. 945	900	40	5
d. 356	300	50	6
e. 476	400	70	6

4. Count the hundreds, tens, and ones, and write the correct numerals in the boxes.

   a. 2 Hundreds 3 Tens 2 Ones
   b. 3 Hundreds 4 Tens 5 Ones
   c. 1 Hundreds 1 Tens 2 Ones
   d. 2 Hundreds 5 Tens 7 Ones

5. Fill in the missing place values.

   a. 451 = 400 + 50 + 1
   b. 763 = 700 + 60 + 3
   c. 564 = 500 + 60 + 4
   d. 132 = 100 + 30 + 2
   e. 678 = 600 + 70 + 8

6. Write the number that is the same as the word.

   a. One hundred five tens four ones   154
   b. Two hundred four tens three ones   243
   c. Six hundreds six tens two ones   662
   d. Seven hundreds four tens six ones   746
   e. Eight hundreds three ones   803

7. Regroup and write the numbers between 0 to 9 in each blank below.

   a. 5 tens + 12 ones = 6 tens + 2 ones
   b. 7 tens + 17 ones = 8 tens + 7 ones
   c. 2 tens + 51 ones = 7 tens + 1 ones
   d. 3 tens + 45 ones = 7 tens + 5 ones
   e. 3 tens + 63 ones = 9 tens + 3 ones

8. Skip count by 5.

a. 120, 125, 130, 135, 140 , 145

b. 235, 240, 245, 250, 255 , 260

c. 615, 620, 625, 630, 635 , 640

d. 540, 545, 550, 555, 560 , 565

e. 780, 785, 790, 795, 800 , 805

9. Skip count by 10 and complete the table.

a.	250	260	270	280	290	300	310
b.	325	335	345	355	365	375	385
c.	810	820	830	840	850	860	870
d.	561	571	581	591	601	611	621
e.	634	644	654	664	674	684	694

10. Skip count by 100s and fill in the missing numbers.

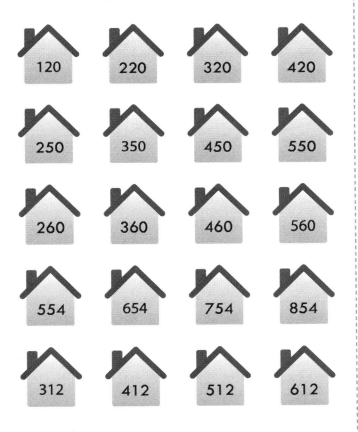

11. Colour the correct answer.

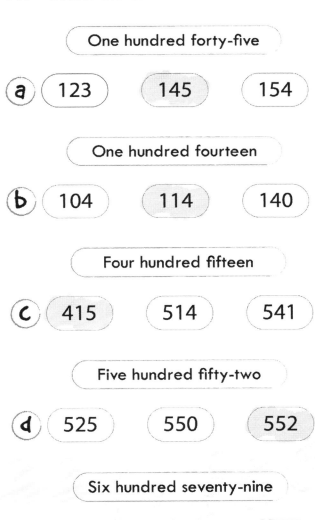

12. Color the correct number name for the number.

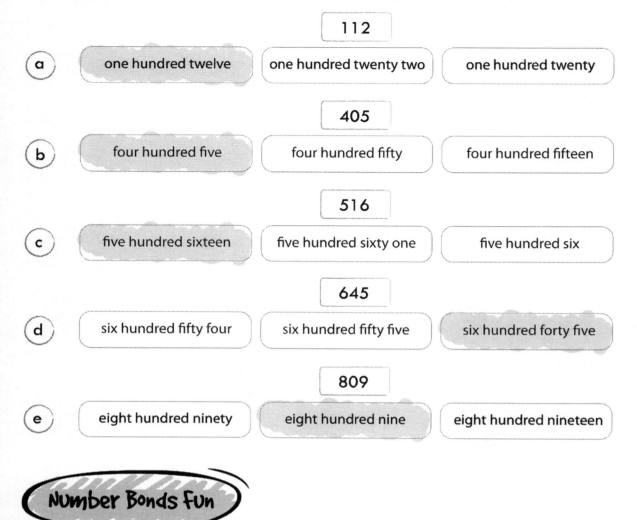

Number Bonds Fun

13. Make number bonds to show the hundreds, tens, and ones in each number. Then write the number in unit form. One is done for you.

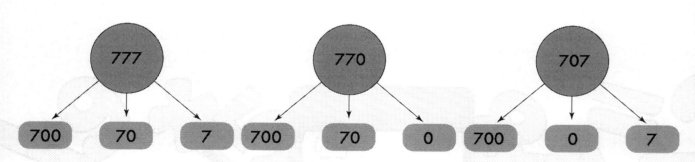

14. Match the number names with the numbers.

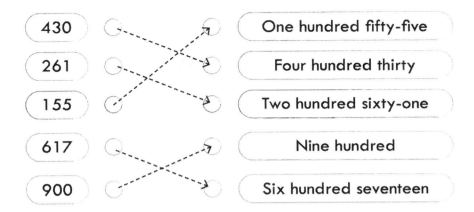

15. Write in standard form or expanded form as stated.

   a. What is 300 + 40 + 5 in standard form? 345

   b. What is 200 + 60 + 1 in standard form? 261

   c. What is 500 + 70 + 8 in standard form? 578

   d. What is 900 + 40 + 3 in standard form? 943

   e. What is 800 + 30 + 1 in standard form? 831

   f. What is the expanded form of 456 ? 400 + 50 + 6

   g. What is the expanded form of 109 ? 100 + 9

   h. What is the expanded form of 578? 500 + 70 + 8

   i. What is the expanded form of 333? 300 + 30 + 3

   j. What is the expanded form of 789? 700 + 80 + 9

16. Match the given standard form with expanded form.

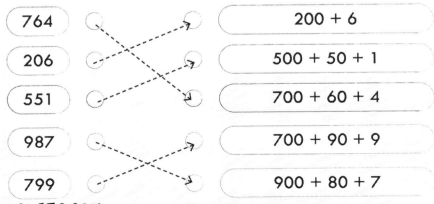

Comparison of Numbers

17. Color the correct word to make each sentence true. Fill in the box with >, < or =.
One is done for you.

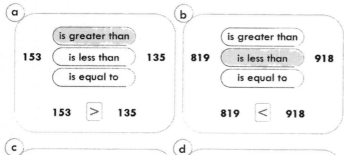

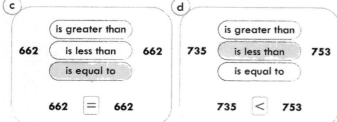

Who is the Greatest?

18. Write the numbers in order from least to greatest.

   a.   123 < 312 < 321
   b.   202 < 220 < 221
   c.   567 < 675 < 765
   d.   823 < 832 < 854

19. Write the numbers in order from greatest to least.

   a.   543 > 534 > 435
   b.   761 > 661 > 617
   c.   998 > 989 > 899
   d.   765 > 734 > 567

Pens and Ice Creams

20. Read the word problems carefully. Write the correct answers in the space provided.

   a. The stationary shop sold the most number of pens in the month of January.

   b. The ice cream shop sold the least number of ice cream cones in the month of June.

21. Solve mentally

   a. 8 ones + 2 ones = 1 ten   8 + 2 = 10
      8 tens + 2 tens = 1 hundred   80 + 20 = 100

   b. 7 ones + 3 ones = 1 ten   7 + 3 = 10
      7 tens + 3 tens = 1 hundred   70 + 30 = 100

c. 1 one + 9 ones = 1 tens $1 + 9 = 10$
    1 ten + 9 tens = 10 tens $10 + 90 = 100$

d. 11 tens + 9 tens = 20 tens $110 + 90 = 200$
    5 ones + 5 ones = 1 ten $5 + 5 = 10$

e. 5 tens + 5 tens = 1 hundred $50 + 50 = 100$
    4 ones + 6 ones = 1 ten $4 + 6 = 10$

f. 4 tens + 6 tens = 1 hundreds $40 + 60 = 100$
    14 tens + 6 tens = 2 hundreds $140 + 60 = 200$

22. Fill in the blanks.

a. 5 ones + 9 ones = 1 tens 4 ones $5 + 9 = 14$
    5 tens + 9 tens = 1 hundreds 4 tens $50 + 90 = 140$

b. 6 ones + 8 ones = 1 tens 4 ones $6 + 8 = 14$
    6 tens + 8 tens = 1 hundreds 4 tens $60 + 80 = 140$

c. 7 ones + 9 ones = 1 tens 6 ones $7 + 9 = 16$
    7 tens + 9 tens = 1 hundreds 6 tens $70 + 90 = 160$

d. 17 ones + 5 ones = 2 tens 2 ones $17 + 5 = 22$
    17 tens + 5 tens = 2 hundreds 2 tens $170 + 50 = 220$

e. 16 ones + 7 ones = 2 tens 3 ones $16 + 7 = 23$
    16 tens + 7 tens = 2 hundreds 3 tens $160 + 70 = 230$

Addition and Subtraction

23. Complete the addition sentence. One is done for you.

a. 25   30   100   d. 18   20   100   200
    25 + 75 = 100   18 + 182 = 200

b. 125   130   200   e. 80   100
    125 + 75 = 200   80 + 20 = 100

c. 6   10   100   f. 76   80   100   200
    6 + 94 = 100   76 + 124 = 200

24. Break apart the addends to find the sum. One is done for you.

b. 54

Add the ones = 9 + 5 = 14 = 1 tens 4 ones
Add the tens = 40 + 10 = 50
How many in all? = 54

c. 58

Add the ones = 9 + 9 = 18 = 1 tens 8 ones
Add the tens = 40 + 10 = 50
How many in all? = 58

d. 100

Add the ones = 5 + 5 = 10 = 1 tens
Add the tens = 50 + 40 + 10 = 100
How many in all? 100

e. 81

Add the ones = 7 + 4 = 11 = 1 tens 1 ones
Add the tens = 60 + 10 + 10 = 80
How many in all? 81

f. 97

Add the ones = 2 + 5 = 7
Add the tens = 80 + 10 = 90
How many in all? 97

25. b. 82
    c. 121
    d. 200
    e. 171

26. b. 19
    c. 65
    d. 143
    e. 100
    f. 190

27. a. (i) 82 bushes were planted.
       (ii) 137 bushes and trees were planted
    b. (i) 50 points
       (ii) 85 points
    c. 934 books
    d. $ 110
    e. 200 pens

28. a. 31
    b. 145
    c. 191
    d. 175
    e. 26
    f. 40
    g. 41
    h. 20

29. b. 23
    c. 111
    d. 321
    e. 342

30. a. 228
    b. 617
    c. 0
    d. 8

31. a. 36
    b. 19
    c. 47
    d. 69
    e. 46
    f. 9

32. No, William is not correct. Explanation might vary

33. a. True
    b. False
    c. True

34. a. 58
    b. Jack saved $18 more than Thompson.
    c. 131 coins

35. a. 143
    b. 168

36. a. 3
    b. 4
    c. 0
    d. 3

37. a. 1 hundred = 10 tens
    b. 20 tens = 2 hundreds
    c. 40 ones = 4 tens
    d. 5 tens = 50 ones

38. Correctly color the numbers as specified.

39. a. 162
    b. 328
    c. 273
    d. 184

40. a. 35 ones = 30 + 5
       70 tens
       30 + 70 tens = 100 tens and 5 ones, thus the number is 105.
    b. 10 + 10 + 10 + 10 + 10 + 10 + 10 + 10 = 80 pennies.
    c. Jack can show the ten twice, thus totalling 20.

41.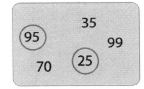
    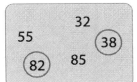 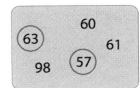

42. a. 111
    b. 79
    c. 156
    d. Kind Tigers and Wales United
    e. Curvy Lions and Smart Horses

43. a. 28 more students
     b. 16 more students
     c. 2 students
45. b. 429
     c. 1060
     d. 182

44. a. 100 beads
     b. 244 stickers
     c. $360
     d. 270 houses

Measurement

1. a. 9 centimeters
    b. 15 centimeters
    c. 11 centimeters
    d. 5 centimeters
    e. 14 centimeters
    f. Stick
    g. Paperclip
    h. Shorter by 10 centimeters
2. Answers will vary

3. a. 12 inch ruler
    b. Yardstick
    c. Yardstick
    d. 12 inch ruler
4. a. 1 meter
    b. 20 centimeters
    c. 2 meters
    d. 15 centimeters

5. a. Answer will vary
    b. Answer will vary
    c. Number of centimeters
    d. Because centimeter is a smaller unit than inch

6. a. 11 inches
    b. Yardstick
    c. 5 inches
    d. Measuring tape
    e. 10 centimeters
7. Answers will vary.
8. 4 feet
    2 inches
    7 feet
9. a. Answer will vary
    b. Answer will vary
    c. Answer will vary
    d. Rectangle
    e. Rectangle, Diamond, Triangle
    f. Answer will vary
    g. Answer will vary

10. a. 5 meters
    b. 6 inches
    c. 93 meters
    d. 7 feet

11. 10 meters

12. a. 58 meters
    b. 31 meters
    c. More metres, since it is the smaller unit.

13. Answers may vary.
    Because they are different units

14. Answers may vary.
    Centimeter. Because the centimeter is smaller than the inch.

15. a. Meters
    b. Centimeters
    c. Centimeters
    d. Meters

16. a. 7 centimeters
    b. 6 centimeters
    c. 8 centimeters

17. a. Feet
    b. Inches
    c. Meters
    d. Inches
    e. Centimeters
    f. Inches

18. a. 3, 1, 2
    b. 2, 3, 1

19. a. 2 inches
    b. 5 yards
    c. 10 feet
    d. 16 yards
    e. 12 meters

20. a. 65 inches
    b. 22 inches

21. a. 8 + 8 + 8 + 8 = 32 inches
    b. 56 - 38 = 18 feet

22. a. 28 + 42 = 70 centimeters
    b. 42 - 28 = 14 centimeters
    c. 70 - 63 = 7 centimeters

23. a. 17 cars

b. 36 marbles

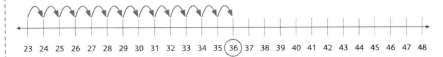

c. 80 children

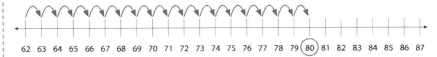

Math with Paper Planes

24. a. 61 centimeters
    b. 84 centimeters
    c. Jasper. 15 centimeters
    d. 8 centimeters

25. 34 meters

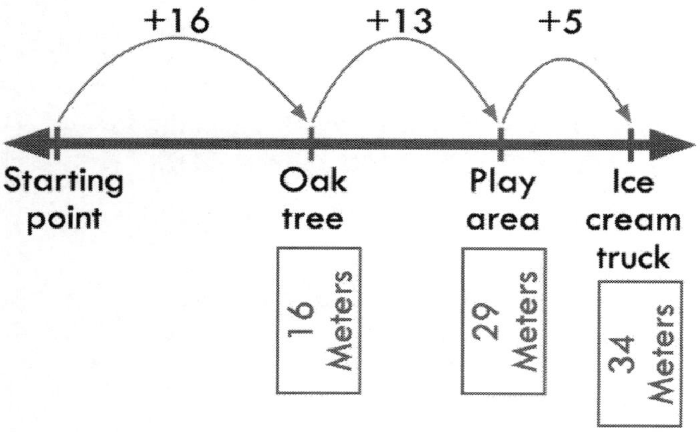

Monday or Tuesday?

26. a. 64 - 32 = 32 degree celsius
    b. 73 - 64 = 9 degree celsius

27. a. 10 centimeters
    b. 8 inches
    c. 12 feet

28. 78 - 43 = 35 meters

29.

a 3 + 17	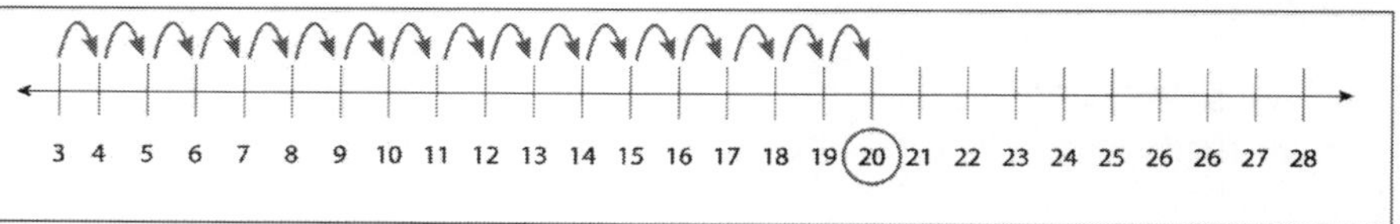
b 4 + 13	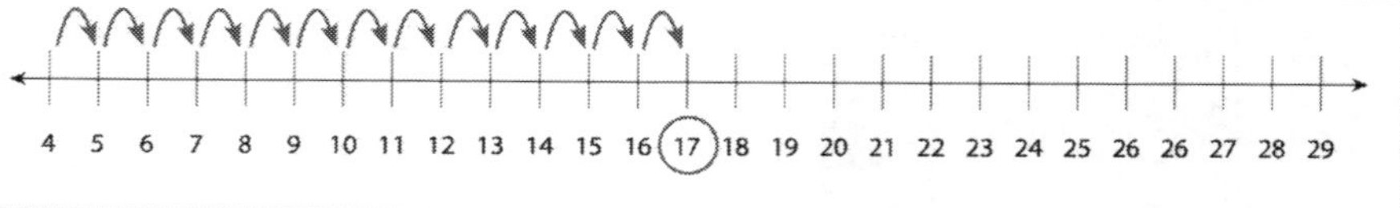
c 15 + 5	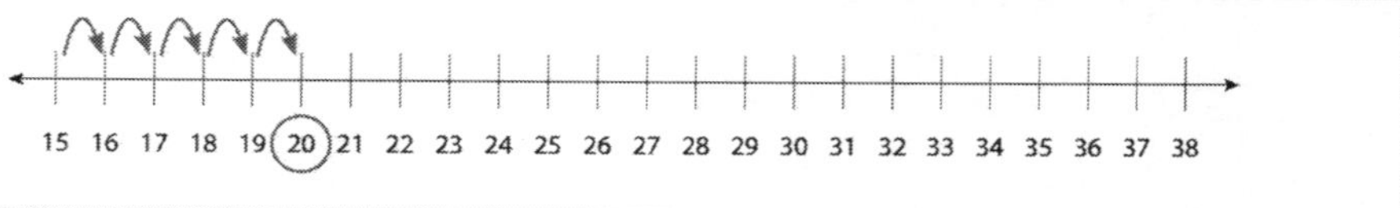
d 13 - 7	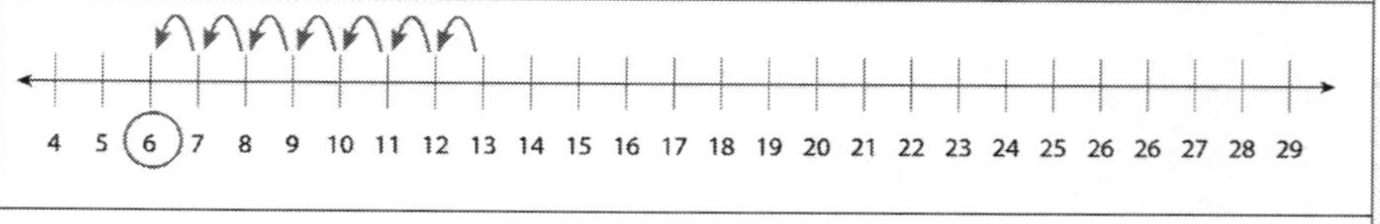
e 19 - 13	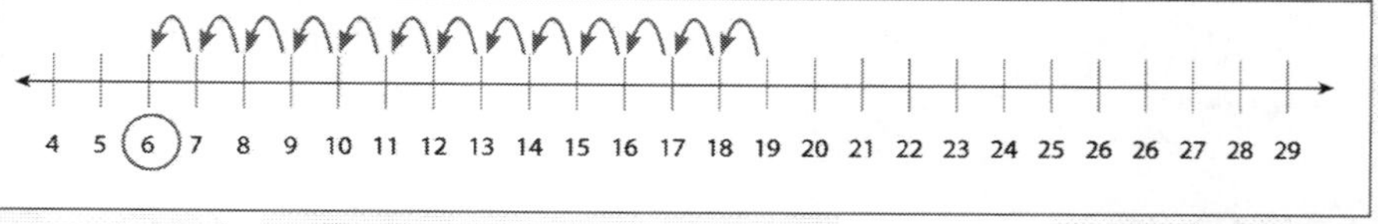

30.

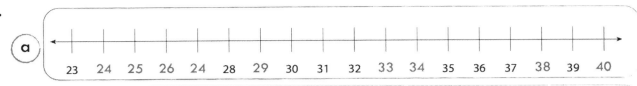

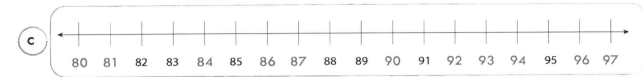

31. 8 + 1 = 9
    10 - 3 = 7

32. a. 4, 5, 6, 7, 8, 9, 10, 11, 12
    b. 8, 10, 12, 14, 16, 18, 20, 22, 24
    c. 20, 25, 30, 35, 40, 45, 50, 55, 60
    d. 40, 50, 60, 70, 80, 90, 100

33. a. 5, 7, 9, 11, 13, 15, 17, 19, 21
    b. 80, 82, 84, 86, 88, 90, 92, 94, 96

34. a. Pricilla will reach first.
    b. 98 - 63 = 35 meters
    c. 63 + 20 = 83 meters

35. Number line a

36. a. 50 - 23 = 27 centimeters
    b. 12 + 17 = 29 centimeters
    c. 5 + 2 = 7 inches

37. a. 40 - 21 = 19 centimeters
    b. 15 + 5 = 20 centimeters
    c. 36 + 11 = 47 inches

38. Inches is a unit of measurement that is greater than centimeters. So 6 inches > 10 centimeters.

39.

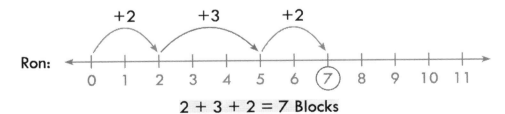

2 + 3 + 2 = 7 Blocks

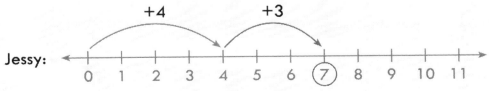

4 + 3 = 7 Blocks

Time

40. Draw the hands to show the time.

3 o'clock   7 o'clock   8 o'clock   10 o'clock

Analogue and Digital Clocks

41. Match the digital clock and the analog clock that show the same time.

42. Read the clock and write the time to the nearest 5 minutes.

1. 1:35   2. 8:10   3. 5:00

43. In a class, students were asked to mark time. Color the correct answer in grey.

| 5:35 | 6:05 | 11:30 |

44.

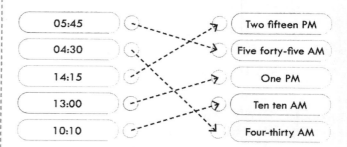

45.

Thirty minutes after four	4:30
Ten minutes to two	1:50
Quarter past eight	8:15
Half-past six	6:30

46. Fill in the blanks with 'AM' or 'PM'.
    a. I went to see the stars at eight PM
    b. I had breakfast at seven AM
    c. I played with my friends at three PM
    d. I wished my parents goodnight at nine PM

Money

Penny, Quarter, Nickel, or Dime

47. a. Nickel
    b. Penny
    c. Quarter
    d. Dime

48. Write the equivalent for each.

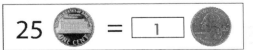

49.
 $ 1.15

 $ 0.81

 $ 1.12

 $ 1

50.
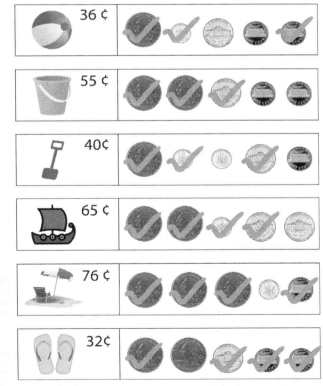

51. Jeff has 11 cents more than Matt.

52. Kim needs to pay $4.00

53. Matt has $1.50 left

54. Sam has $1.50 left

55. a. 10 cents make a dime
    b. 5 nickels make a quarter
    c. 10 dimes make a dollar

Data

Oranges, Apples, and Pomegranate

56.

10	3	4

57. Picture graph to be created in the grid.
    a. 6
    b. 26
    c. 2

Favorite Pet

58. Picture graph to be created in the grid.
    Dog - 14; Cat - 10; Fish - 4
    a. 10
    b. 6
    c. Answers may vary

Sam's Snack Corner

59. Bar graph to be created in the grid.

60. Shirley - 8; Linda - 14
    a. A tape diagram to show the subtraction statement 14 - 8 = 6
    b. 14 + 8 = 22; 32 - 22 = 10; Noah read 10 books.

61. a. 7
    b. 5
    c. Parrot
    d. 46
    e. 46 + 5 = 51

62. a. 36 pennies
    b. 36 - 18 = 18 pennies
    c. 6 pennies
    d. The total amount would increase by 15 and thus the total amount saved would be 36 + 15 = 51 pennies
    e. Answers may vary

What's Your Favourite Musical Instrument?

63. a. 120
    b. Saxophone and trumpet

    c. 10
    d. 30

64. A line graph with the following frequency.
    41 inches - 7
    42 inches - 10
    43 inches - 4
    44 inches - 5
    45 inches - 4

65. a. 11 pounds
    b. 21.5 pounds
    c 4 pounds
    d. Between Week 6 and week 7
    e. 4 pounds

Geometry

Shapes

1.

Octagon   Square   Pentagon

Rectangle   Hexagon   Triangle

2. a. Cube
    b. Cylinder
    c. Cone
    d. Sphere
    e. Rectangular Solid
    f. Pyramid

Square Corners

3. a. 0
    b. 0
    c. 2
    d. 4
    e. 1

4. a. 1/2
    b. 1/3
    c. 2/4
    d. 4/8

Corners and Sides

5. a. Number of sides = 6
       Number of corners = 6
   b. Number of sides = 3
       Number of corners = 3
   c. Number of sides = 4
       Number of corners = 4
   d. Number of sides = 4
       Number of corners = 4
   e. Number of sides = 4
       Number of corners = 4
   f. Number of sides = 0
       Number of corners = 0

6.

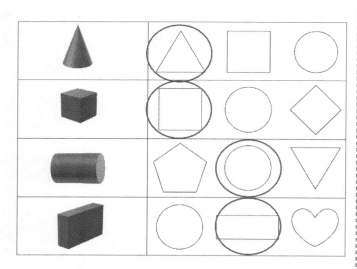

7.

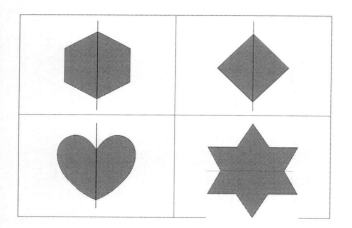

8. a. Yes   e. No
    b. No   f. Yes
    c. No
    d. Yes

9. a. There are 4 circles.
       2 circles are shaded.
       Write the fraction for the shaded part. 2/4
    b. There are 3 triangles.
       1 triangle is shaded.
       Write the fraction for the shaded part. 1/3

10. Answers may vary

11. a, d, e

12. a. Square
    b. Triangle
    c. Octagon
    d. Circle

13. a. 7
    b. 9

14. a. 6

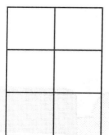

b. 10

15. a. One-half
    b. One-third
    c. One-fourth
    d. Three-fourths
    e. Three-fifths
    f. One-sixth
    g. One-eighth

Equal Shares

16.

a. 2 Halves

b. 3 thirds

c. 4 fourths

17. a.

b.

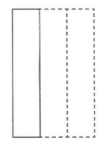

c. One-fourth of a rectangle is given. Make it whole by completing the picture

Pizza Math

18. a. 1/4 one-fourth
    b. 3/4 three-fourth
    c. 1/5 one-fifth

19. a. One-halves

    b.

20. a. 3
    b. 2
    c. 4

Science Answer Key

Sample responses:
- The girl is sitting on the chair.
- The baby is in the pool.
- The baby is near the balloon.
- The horse is jumping over the fence.

- Push, because the cyclist pedals in forward direction
- Push, because the girl moves the door away from her
- Pull, because the boy is pulling the stones to lift himself up
- Push, because the body is moving away from the floor
- Pull, because the lady is moving the baggage towards her
- Push, because the people are moving the cart away

Effects of Force

- Move or stop
- Change direction
- Move or stop
- Change shape
- Change shape
- Move or stop, change direction

Attraction or Repulsion?

- Attract - opposite poles
- Repel - like poles
- Repel - like poles
- Attract - opposite poles
- Repel - like poles
- Attract - opposite poles
- Attract - opposite poles
- Repel - like poles

Types of Simple Machines

1. Lever, Inclined plane, Wheel, Inclined plane, Lever

True or False?

1. False. It holds us (humans) and every other living and non-living thing closer to its surface.
2. True. Bigger the object, stronger the gravity.
3. False. There is gravity for everything.
4. True.
5. False. It falls down because of the Earth's gravity whis is stronger than the ball's gravity.

Types of Sounds

1. Snap fingers - soft
2. Playing drums - loud
3. A barking dog - loud
4. A duck's quack - soft
5. Knocking on the door - soft
6. People on a roller coaster - loud

Gravity vs Friction

1. Gravity - makes the apple fall to the ground
2. Friction - helps cycling uphill
3. Gravity - enables smooth movement
4. Friction - enables controlled motion
5. Gravity - makes the ball come back to the ground
6. Gravity - causes the fall and breakage of Humpty Dumpty

Uses of Friction

1. Useful, because the cycle will skid if there is no friction
2. Useful, because our hands will slip when we push up without friction
3. Not useful, because friction will slow down the wheels of the baggage
4. Useful because the players will trip and fall in the absence of friction
5. Not useful, because friction will not allow us to roll freely
6. Useful, because absence of friction will not make the snap. Try snapping with oily fingers.

www.prepaze.com

Energy Word Grid

1. Sound
2. Position
3. Push
4. Speed
5. Distance
6. Pull
7. Motion
8. Friction
9. Soft
10. Wheel
11. Lever
12. Direction

W	H	E	E	L	O	D	P	W	S
S	E	F	F	J	A	I	O	I	O
P	J	R	W	Q	V	S	S	S	U
E	D	I	R	E	C	T	I	O	N
E	E	C	P	U	S	A	T	F	D
D	P	T	U	V	V	N	I	T	I
X	U	I	L	M	C	C	O	B	E
V	S	O	L	H	W	E	N	A	V
E	H	N	T	V	N	Y	U	K	E
M	O	T	I	O	N	Y	Q	X	R

Name the Young Ones

Pup, kitten, calf, chick, duckling, larva, lamb, fawn, foal, gosling

Animals and Their Young Ones

Reproduction in Animals

1. Egg laying
2. Giving birth to young ones
3. Giving birth to young ones
4. Egg laying

Reproduction in Plants

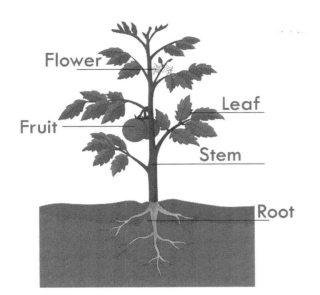

Germination

Seed, Root, Shoot, Cotyledons

Lifecycle of a Plant

Seed, Sapling, Plant, Flower, Fruit

Modes of Seed Dispersal

Seeds → **Mode of dispersal**

- ANIMALS
- EXPLOSION
- WIND
- WATER

Lifecycle of a Butterfly

1. Egg
2. Larva
3. Pupa
4. Butterfly

Lifecycle of a Frog

Eggs, tadpole, froglet, frog

Minerals

1. Feldspar
2. Mica
3. Fluorite
4. Quartz
5. Gold
6. Copper
7. Talc
8. Aluminium

Properties of Minerals

1. Diamond - hard, shiny
2. Lead - soft, shiny
3. Quartz - hard, shiny
4. Copper - hard, shiny
5. Gold - soft, shiny

Agents of Weathering

Water, wind, wind, water, plant

Identify the Minerals

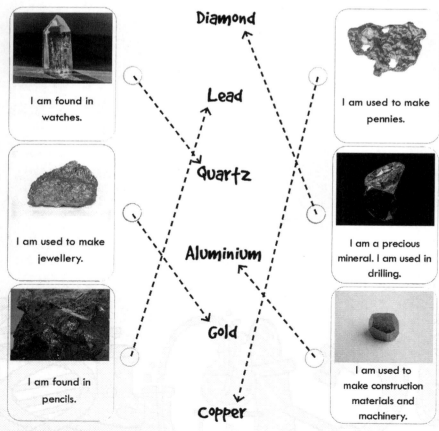

Kinds of Soil

What does the soil look like?			
Name of the soil	**Red Soil**	**Sand**	**Top Soil**
Colour of the soil	☐ Light brown ☐ Dark brown ☒ Red ☐ Black	☒ Light brown ☐ Dark brown ☐ Red ☐ Black	☐ Light brown ☒ Dark brown ☐ Red ☒ Black
Texture	☒ Clay ☐ Clumpy ☐ Grainy	☐ Clay ☐ Clumpy ☒ Grainy	☐ Clay ☒ Clumpy ☐ Grainy
Water retention	☐ High ☒ Low	☐ High ☒ Low	☒ High ☐ Low
What does it have?	☒ Iron ☐ Tiny bits of plants ☐ Tiny bits of animals ☒ Grainy bits of rocks	☐ Iron ☐ Tiny bits of plants ☒ Tiny bits of animals ☒ Grainy bits of rocks	☐ Iron ☒ Tiny bits of plants ☒ Tiny bits of animals ☒ Grainy bits of rocks
Growth of plants	☒ Not much ☐ Most plants ☐ Few plants	☐ Not much ☐ Most plants ☒ Few plants	☐ Not much ☒ Most plants ☐ Few plants

Fossil Questionnaire

1. Paleontologist
2. Extinct
3. Skeleton
4. Mammoth
5. Fossil
6. Millions of years
7. Disease, natural disasters
8. Rancho La Brea
9. Ankylosaur
10. Geologist

Sources of Food

Plant products: Bread, Eggplant, Wheat, Apple, Potato, Mushroom, Broccoli,

Animal Products: Egg, Milk, Chicken, Honey, Cheese, Fish, Shrimp, Butter, Beef

Uses of Natural Resources

Tree - Wood - Furniture
Water - Energy - Electricity
Mountain - Minerals - Jewelry
Soil - Crop - Food
Wind - Energy - Electricity
Animal - Wool - Clothes

Bar Graph

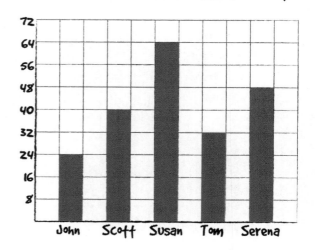

Make Predictions

Growing Conditions		Prediction
Water	Sunlight	(What do you think will happen?)
✓	✓	☒ The seed will germinate and grow well ☐ The seed will germinate, may or may not grow well ☐ The seed will not germinate
✓	✗	☐ The seed will germinate and grow well ☒ The seed will germinate, may or may not grow well ☐ The seed will not germinate
✗	✓	☐ The seed will germinate and grow well ☐ The seed will germinate, may or may not grow well ☒ The seed will not germinate
✗	✗	☐ The seed will germinate and grow well ☐ The seed will germinate, may or may not grow well ☒ The seed will not germinate

www.prepaze.com

prepaze

www.aceacademicpublishing.com

THE ONE BIG BOOK

GRADE 2

For English, Math, and Science

Ace Academic Publishing
ACHIEVING EXCELLENCE TOGETHER

Printed in Poland
by Amazon Fulfillment
Poland Sp. z o.o., Wrocław